Better Homes and Gardens®

A Cross-Stitch
CHRISTMAS®

Celebrations in Stitches

Elizabeth M. Burd

June 2001

Better Homes and Gardens® Creative Collection
Des Moines, Iowa

Better Homes and Gardens.

A Cross-Stitch
CHRISTMAS®

Editor-in-Chief Beverly Rivers

Creatve Director Daniel Masini
Senior Editor Eve Mahr
Associate Art Director Patty Crawford

Editorial Coordinator Carol Linnan
Editorial Project Coordinator Barbara Hickey
Editorial Assistant Mary Johnson
Contributing Writers Laura Collins, Rhonda Mattus, Kris Petersen
Copy Editors Debra Morris Smith, Margaret Smith
Contributing Illustrators Marcia Cameron, Chris Neubauer Graphics

Publishing Director William R. Reed
Publisher Maureen Ruth
Group Consumer Marketing Director Liz Bredeson
Marketing Manager Becky Nash
Business Manager Kristin Eaton
Production Director Douglas M. Johnston
Book Production Managers Pam Kvitne, Marjorie J. Schenkelberg

Vice President
Jerry Ward

CORPORATION

Chairman and CEO
William T. Kerr

Chairman of the Executive Committee
E.T. Meredith III

Meredith Publishing Group

Publishing Group President Stephen M. Lacy
Magazine Group President Jerry Kaplan
Group Sales Michael Brownstein
Creative Services Ellen de Lathouder
Manufacturing Bruce Heston
Consumer Marketing Karla Jeffers
Operations Dean Pieters
Finance and Administration Max Runciman

Member

HiA
**HOBBY INDUSTRY
ASSOCIATION**

Our Mark of Excellence seal assures you
that every project in this book has been
constructed and checked under the direction of
the cross-stitch experts at *Better Homes and
Gardens® Creative Collection™*.

For book editorial questions, write
Better Homes and Gardens® A Cross-Stitch Christmas
1716 Locust St.–GA 307,
Des Moines, IA 50309-3023;
phone 515/284-3623; fax 515/284-3045.
For additional copies or billing questions,
call 800/322-0691.

First Edition. Printing Number and Year: 5 4 3 2 1   04 03 02 01
ISSN: 1081-468X
ISBN: 0-696-21363-X

Cross-stitchers celebrate Christmas in extraordinary ways. They know the joy of creating handmade ornaments, personalized gifts, and beautiful home accessories. Some elect to make a Christmas pièce de résistance, choosing patterns, fabrics, and threads and completing a major project long before the holiday season debuts. Others wait and opt for one-night wonders or make quick-to-stitch designs for late-list additions. Many find stitching a refuge from stress and the hectic pace of Christmas preparations.

Whatever your stitching style, this collection of Christmas cross-stitch designs was written just for you. We've chosen beautiful holiday pieces you'll want to display all year, marvelous gifts for everyone on your list, amazing ornaments for every tree size, and attractive accessories that say "Merry Christmas" throughout the house. To help make your holiday stitching personal, our designers turned their imaginations loose with extra projects, fabric options, and ideas to spur your creativity.

As you enjoy Christmas with projects from this book, may your holidays be

Celebrations in Stitches.

A CROSS-STITCH CHRISTMAS.
Contents

62 Stitched for Giving

Stitch the best gifts with your heart—and your hands.

82 Traditions Renewed

Refresh the holiday routine with old-time Christmas customs and icons.

104 Tree Trimmings

Dress your tannenbaum in lovingly stitched ornaments and trims.

Christmas

Carols

At Christmas let your heart and home sing with holiday stitches. Based on five cherished melodies, this musical sampler captures refrains on everything from framed pictures and hand towels to a Christmas stocking, package tie-on, and greeting card. Solemn and stately or bright and cheery, all ring through the house in harmony and good Christmas measure.

What a glorious symphony of fonts!

Setting forth the centuries-old German carol, Lo, How a Rose, *the framed piece,* opposite, *almost sings. Rose "flow'rets," symbolic of the coming of the Christ Child, illuminate the piece and lend themselves to smaller gift ideas, too. Try a flowering garland for the towel band or the tiny wreath on a gift tag. For the soft look of the towel banding, stitch any of the designs with overdyed threads.*

Project instructions begin on page 14.
Design: BrightNeedle Charted Designs. Photographs: Perry Struse

*T*he lively tale of Frosty the Snowman *delights kids as much today as it did in 1953 when Perry Como first recorded the tune. To melt hearts throughout the holidays, catch Frosty's happy image framed with a checkerboard border on a 9-inch square pillow.*

Project instructions begin on page 19.
Design: Kathy Moenkhaus. Photograph: Scott Little

*J*ust who wrote the music and lyrics *to* I Saw Three Ships, opposite, *remains a mystery to us. Yet thanks to generations of English carolers, the beloved refrain lives on in our hearts and voices today, inspiring these adventuresome pieces. Three ships embark upon a sea of cross-stitches for the Christmas stocking, opposite. The largest of the nautical trio makes waves on a treasure box.*

Project instructions begin on page 16.
Design: Robin Clark. Photographs: Marcia Cameron and Scott Little

It's Beginning to Look Like Christmas

shares a common composer, Meredith Willson, with Broadway's
The Music Man. *This quick-to-stitch design captures his
lighthearted holiday tune in a pair of enthusiastic carolers. Worked
in backstitching, crosses, and buttons, the duo belts out the song's
memorable words as charmed notes and snowflakes fill the air. Even
the tree is "charmed" with yarn-textured branches.*

Project instructions begin on page 20.
Design: Annie Lippincott. Photograph: Steve Struse

Phillips Brooks, an Episcopal priest from

*Philadelphia, journeyed through the Holy Land during the
Christmas of 1865. Awestruck by his experiences, he eventually
put his memories into the verse* O Little Town of Bethlehem.
*Make a gift of a scene much like the one that inspired Brooks' carol so long ago, shepherds keeping vigil
as night falls over Bethlehem, opposite. Or, stitch a single shepherd and lamb gazing at a gilded star for
the very special greeting.*

Project instructions begin on page 22.
Design: Mari McDonald for Whispered in the Wind. Photograph: Marcia Cameron

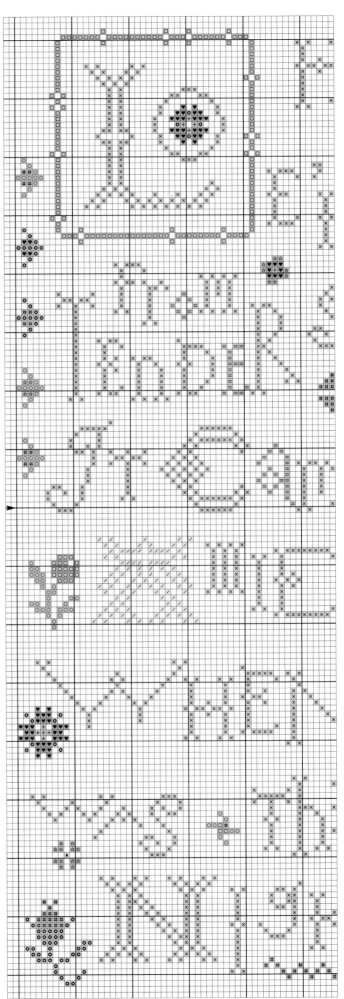

Lo, How a Rose Sampler

Anchor		DMC	Weeks Dye Works	
855	O	370 Pecan	1201	Putty
860	⊙	522 Olive drab	2196	Scuppernong
1040	=	647 True beaver gray	1151	Pebble
900	/	648 Light beaver gray	1174	Tin roof
8581	X	3022 Brown-gray	1198	London Fog
059	♥	3350 Dusty rose	2279	Sweetheart rose
1027	□	3722 Shell pink	2278	Hibiscus
1019	☆	3726 Antique mauve	1139	Chablis
1048	◆	3826 Golden brown	1224	Amber
901	+	3829 Old gold	2221	Gold
339	⊞	3830 Terra-cotta	2254	Cinnabar

Stitch count: *88 high x 42 wide*
Finished design sizes:
27-count fabric – 6½ x 3⅛ inches
28-count fabric – 6¼ x 3 inches
32-count fabric – 5½ x 2⅝ inches

Lo, How a Rose Sampler

The chart and key are on pages 14–15.

supplies

17" square of 32-count antique white
  Belfast linen
Cotton embroidery floss
Desired frame

stitches

Center and stitch the chart on the linen.
Use two plies of floss to work the
stitches over two threads of the fabric
unless otherwise specified. Press the
stitched piece from the back. Frame
as desired.

Rose Package Tie

The chart and key are on pages 14–15.

supplies

6" square of 14-count cream perforated
  paper
Cotton embroidery floss
Mill Hill Crystal Treasures red heart
  (13042)
2⅝×6" cream decorative paper
2⅝" square of tan decorative paper
Glue
Scallop-edge scissors (optional)

stitches

Center and stitch the octagonal rose
motif indicated by the dotted line on
the Lo, How a Rose chart onto the
paper. Use two plies of floss to work
the cross-stitches over one square. Work
the remaining stitches as specified in the
key. Attach the heart charm using two
plies of floss.

assembly

Trim the stitched piece one square
beyond the stitching. Glue the trimmed
piece to the 2⅝" square of tan paper. If
desired, trim one end of the cream paper
with scallop-edge scissors. Referring to
the photograph *below*, glue the tan paper
to the cream paper.

Rose Vine Towels

The chart and key are on pages 14–15.

supplies

For each towel
3"-wide 27-count Celeste linen banding
  2" longer than the width of the towel
Weeks Dyeworks overdyed floss
⅛"-wide hand-dyed silk ribbon, double
  the width of the towel plus 4"
Purchased towel
Matching sewing thread

stitches

Measure in 1" from a short edge of the
banding; begin stitching one end of the
rosebud vine, indicated by the dotted
line on the Lo, How a Rose chart,
there. Center the vine horizontally on
the banding. Use two plies of floss to
work the stitches over two threads.
When working with overdyed floss,
complete each cross-stitch before beginning the next. Repeat the chart as needed,
stopping 1" from the end of the banding.
Press the banding from the back.

assembly

Cut the ribbon in half and thread each
piece through the eyelets in the banding.
Pin the banding on the towel. Fold the
banding ends under so they are even
with the towel edges. Machine- or
hand-sew the banding in place.

I Saw Three Ships Stocking

supplies

18×15" piece of 14-count dusty miller
  Aida cloth
Cotton embroidery floss
Graph paper; pencil
14×10" piece of fusible fleece
Erasable fabric marker
⅜ yard of 45"-wide coordinating cotton
  fabric
1½ yards of ⅛"-diameter cording
Matching sewing thread

stitches

Use the alphabet on *page 18* to chart the
desired name on graph paper, separating
each letter with one square.

  Center and stitch the chart on the
fabric. Use three plies of floss to work
the stitches over one square of the fabric
unless otherwise specified. Press the
stitched piece from the back.

assembly

Center and fuse the fleece to the back
of the stitched piece following the
manufacturer's instructions. Use the
erasable fabric marker to draw the
stocking outline around the stitched area
of the design as indicated by the dotted

continued

I Saw Three Ships Stocking

Anchor		DMC
002	·	000 White
897	O	221 Shell pink
683	X	500 Deep blue-green
878	∧	501 Dark blue-green
045	▲	814 Garnet
838	◫	926 Medium gray-blue
837	◎	927 Light gray-blue
862	◆	934 Pine green
905	✳	3021 Deep brown-gray
8581	▽	3022 Medium brown-gray
900	—	3024 Pale brown-gray
887	✳	3045 Dark yellow-beige
886	▯	3046 Medium yellow-beige
681	✚	3051 Gray-green
840	▦	3768 Dark gray-blue
1007	⊕	3772 Cocoa
904	✚	3787 Dark brown-gray

BACKSTITCH (1X)
905	╱	3021 Deep brown-gray –
		all stitches

Stitch count: 178 high x 131 wide
Finished design sizes:
14-count fabric – 12¾ x 9⅓ inches
16-count fabric – 11⅛ x 8⅛ inches
18-count fabric – 9⅞ x 7¼ inches

With right sides facing, sew the lining pieces together with a ½" seam allowance, leaving the top edge open and an opening on one side for turning. Trim the seams and clip the curves, but *do not* turn. Slip the stocking inside the lining with right sides together. Use the zipper foot to sew around the top edge of the stocking. Trim the seam and turn right side out. Slip-stitch the opening closed. Tuck the lining into the stocking and press carefully.

Sailing Ship Box

supplies
8" square of 18-count Rustico Aida cloth
Cotton embroidery floss
Purchased 5" square oak box with
    3¼" opening

stitches
Center and stitch the center ship from the I Saw Three Ships Stocking chart onto the fabric. Use two plies of floss to work the cross-stitches over one square of fabric unless otherwise specified. Press the stitched piece from the back. Mount it in the box lid following manufacturer's instructions.

line on the chart. Cut out the stocking shape ½" beyond the marked outline.

Use the trimmed stitched piece as a pattern to cut a matching back and two lining pieces from the coordinating fabric. Also cut a 4½×1½" hanging strip and enough 1½"-wide bias strips to make 54" of piping from the coordinating fabric.

Sew the short ends of the piping strips together to make one long strip. Center the cording lengthwise on the wrong side of the piping strip. Fold the fabric around the cording with the long edges together. Use a zipper foot to sew through both layers close to the cording. Baste the piping around the sides and foot of the stocking front with the raw edges even.

With right sides together and using the zipper foot, sew the stocking front to the back along the basting lines, leaving the top edge open. Trim the seams, clip the curves, and turn right side out. Press.

With raw edges even, baste piping around the top edges of the stocking. Press under ⅜" on the long edges of the hanging strip, fold it in half lengthwise and topstitch. Fold the strip in half to form a loop. Sew the loop to the top right corner of the stocking with the raw edges even.

I Saw Three Ships Numbers

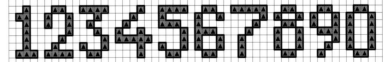

I Saw Three Ships Alphabet

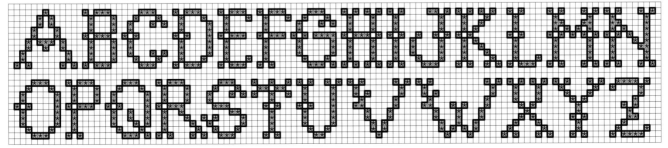

Frosty the Snowman Pillow

Frosty the Snowman Pillow

Anchor		DMC	
897	♥	221	Deep shell pink
1026	–	225	Pale shell pink
900	○	648	Beaver gray
339	◉	920	Copper
1034	✕	931	Medium antique blue
905	◆	3021	Brown-gray
896	▦	3721	Dark shell pink
1036	●	3750	Deep antique blue
1048	▢	3776	Mahogany

BLENDED-NEEDLE STRAIGHT STITCH

218	/	319 Dark pistachio (1X) and
215		320 True pistachio (1X) and
244		987 Forest green (1X)

Stitch count: 105 high x 105 wide
Finished design sizes:
28-count fabric – 7½ x 7½ inches
32-count fabric – 6⅔ x 6⅔ inches
36-count fabric – 5⅞ x 5⅞ inches

Frosty the Snowman Pillow

supplies
14" square of 28-count antique white Jobelan fabric
Cotton embroidery floss
⅜ yard of blue print cotton fabric
1¼ yards of ¼"-diameter cording
Matching sewing thread
Polyester fiberfill

continued

stitches

Center and stitch the chart on the Jobelan fabric. Use two plies of floss to work the stitches over two threads of the fabric unless otherwise specified. Press the stitched piece from the back.

assembly

Centering the design, trim the stitched piece to a 10" square. From the blue print fabric, cut a 10" square for the back and enough 1¾"-wide bias strips to make 45" of piping. All measurements include a ½" seam allowance.

Sew the short ends of the 1¾"-wide bias piping strips together to make one long piece. Center the cording lengthwise on the wrong side of the piping strip. Fold the fabric around the cording with the long edges together. Use a zipper foot to sew through both layers close to the cording. With the raw edges even, baste the piping to the front of the stitched piece, overlapping the ends at the center bottom.

Sew the pillow front and back together with right sides facing, slightly rounding the corners and leaving an opening for turning. Trim the seams, clip the corners, and turn right side out. Press. Stuff the pillow firmly with polyester fiberfill and slip-stitch the opening closed.

It's Beginning to Look Like Christmas

supplies

6 tea bags
15" square of Osnaburg fabric
Tracing paper
Iron-on transfer pen
Cotton embroidery floss
Green Papieretto novelty thread
Chenille and ribbon embroidery needles
6—¼"-diameter black buttons
3 Mill Hill Treasures snowflakes
 (#15001)
¾"-tall red ceramic star button
¼"-tall red ceramic star
1½"-diameter round ecru doily
Fine-tip black marking pen
Crafts glue
Desired frame

Stem stitch

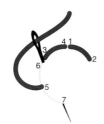

Backstitch curve

French knot

Satin stitch

Straight stitch

stitches

To tea-dye the fabrics, pour very hot water over the tea bags; let steep for about 20 minutes. Remove the tea bags and stir well. Dip the Osnaburg fabric square and doily into the warm tea and let them soak. Stir the tea and check the fabric and doily every five minutes until they reach the color desired. The color will appear lighter when dry than when wet.

When the fabric and doily reach the desired color, remove them from the bath and squeeze out the excess tea. Let the items air dry and then press the pieces from the back.

Trace the pattern, *opposite,* onto the tracing paper using the iron-on transfer pen. Center the traced pattern, ink side down, on the fabric and transfer following the manufacturer's instructions. Work all stitches as specified.

For the tree branches, thread a ribbon embroidery needle with one strand of Papieretto thread and make long ½"-long backstitches. After completing the outline, use the needle to pull the raggedy ends of the thread to the front of the fabric. Trim the thread ends to desired lengths.

Attach the black buttons, snowflakes, and the ¾" star button with two plies of matching floss as indicated on the pattern. Referring to the photograph, *above,* cut the doily for the collar. Position the collar along the girl's chin; sew the top edge of the collar to the fabric. Glue the ¼" star to the top center of the collar. Frame as desired.

It's Beginning to Look Like Christmas

Anchor | DMC

STEM STITCH (3X)
360 ╱ 898 Coffee brown – tree trunk

BACKSTITCH (2X)
403 ╱ 310 Black – musical notes, mouth outlines
235 ╱ 318 Steel – head outlines
307 ╱ 783 Christmas gold – girl's coat
045 ╱ 814 Garnet – boy's scarf and lettering
1036 ╱ 3750 Antique blue – boy's sweater
╱ Papieretto green novelty thread – branches (1X)

Anchor | DMC

STRAIGHT STITCH (2X)
403 ╱ 310 Black – ear detail
045 ╱ 814 Garnet – small x's on boy's scarf
360 ╱ 898 Coffee brown – large X's on girl's coat

SATIN STITCH (2X)
403 ▤ 310 Black – mouths

Anchor | DMC

FRENCH KNOT
403 ● 310 Black – nostrils (2X wrapped twice), freckles (1X wrapped once)
045 ● 814 Garnet – lettering (2X wrapped twice)

SURFACE ATTACHMENTS
⌣ Lace doily
✦ Extra small red star button
✦ Small narrow red star button
✳ 15001 Mill Hill white snowflake
⬤ ⅛"-diameter black buttons

O Little Town of Bethlehem

supplies

14" square of 32-count sage Jobelan
Cotton embroidery floss
Kreinik blending filament
Kreinik # 4 very fine braid
Rainbow Gallery Whisper thread
Desired frame

stitches

Center and stitch the chart on the Jobelan. Use two plies of floss to work the stitches over two threads of the fabric unless otherwise specified. Press the stitched piece from the back. Frame as desired.

Shepherd and Lamb Greeting Card

supplies

4×6" piece of 14-count white Aida cloth
Cotton embroidery floss
Light yellow beige (DMC 3047) cotton embroidery floss
¾"-diameter star-shape rubber stamp
Gold stamp pad
Gold embossing powder
Embossing or other heating tool
4¼×3" piece of fusible interfacing
Purchased 3⅛×4½" greeting card with 2½×4" rectangular opening
Tape

stitches

Center and stitch the portion of the O Little Town of Bethlehem chart indicated by the dotted line onto the fabric, substituting light yellow beige for the lamb's body. Use three plies of floss to work the cross-stitches over one square of the fabric. Work the backstitches as specified on the key. Press the stitched piece from the back.

assembly

Use the rubber stamp and pad to stamp a star in the upper right-hand corner of the front of the card. While the ink is wet, shake embossing powder over it, tapping excess powder back into the jar. Hold the card over an embossing tool until the powder melts; cool. (Or, carefully hold the card above a hair dryer, electric stove burner, or toaster.) Center and fuse the interfacing to the back of the stitched piece, following manufacturer's instructions. Trim the edges of the stitched piece even with the interfacing. Center and tape to the backside of the card front.

O Little Town of Bethlehem

Anchor	DMC	
370	434	Chestnut
860	522	Dark olive drab
859	523	Medium olive drab
858	524	Light olive drab
889	610	Drab brown
273	645	Dark beaver gray
845	730	Olive
360	839	Dark beige-brown
378	841	True beige-brown
851	924	Deep gray-blue
850	926	Medium gray-blue
849	927	Light gray-blue
274	928	Pale gray-blue
779	931	Medium antique blue
861	935	Dark pine green
846	936	Medium pine green
1012	948	Peach
369	976	Golden brown
844	3012	Khaki
871	3041	Medium antique violet
870	3042	Light antique violet
888	3045	Yellow-beige
872	3740	Dark antique violet
869	3743	Pale antique violet
848	3752	Light antique blue
1050	3781	Mocha
	032	Kreinik Pearl #4 very-fine braid

Anchor	DMC	
BLENDED-NEEDLE		
001	B5200	White white (1X) and
	W88	Rainbow Gallery Whisper white (1X)
001	B5200	White white (1X) and
	032	Kreinik Pearl blending filament (1X)
8581	646	Medium beaver gray (1X) and
	W88	Rainbow Gallery Whisper white (1X)
779	931	Medium antique blue (1X) and
851	924	Deep gray-blue (1X)
1040	3022	Medium brown-gray (1X) and
	W88	Rainbow Gallery Whisper white (1X)
BACKSTITCH		
360	839	Dark beige-brown – tree trunk detail (1X)
779	931	Medium antique blue – horizon line (1X)
861	935	Dark pine green – branches on palm trees in background (1X); grass blades (2X)
5975	3830	Terra-cotta – face, hands, and feet (1X)
STRAIGHT STITCH		
001	B5200	White white (1X) and
	032	Kreinik Pearl blending filament (1X)

Stitch count: 94 high x 122 wide

Finished design sizes:
32-count fabric – 5⅞ x 7⅝ inches
28-count fabric – 6¾ x 8¾ inches
36-count fabric – 5¾ x 6¾ inches

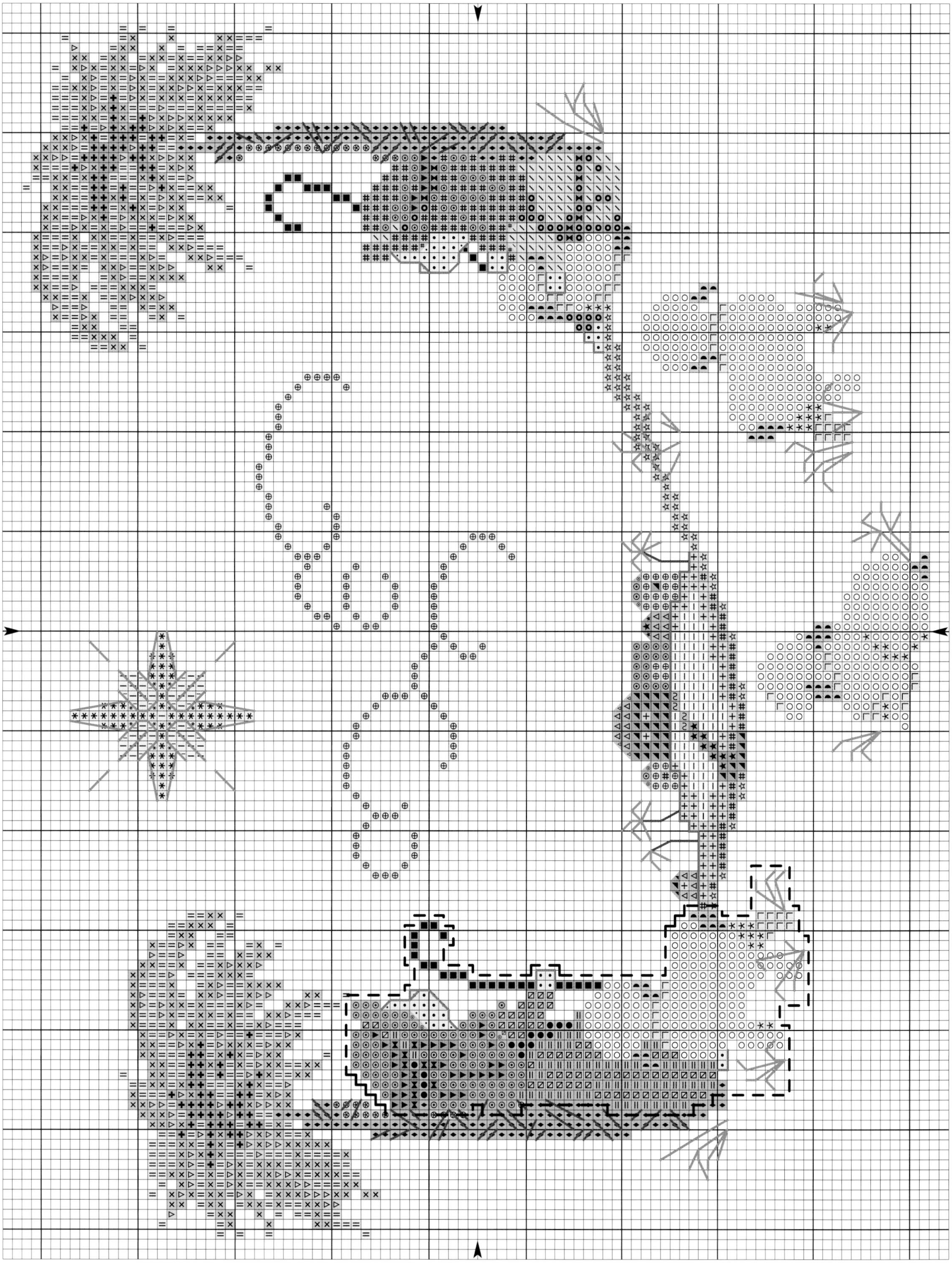

Holiday

Memories

Christmas memories mellow over time, but they never grow old in our hearts. A fresh sense of wonder fills us each time familiar decorations take their places in our homes. For this selection, we've chosen remembrances from the past and incorporated them into new treasures to enjoy this season and for many Christmases to come.

*F*rom its rum-tummy-tum drum base
to the tip of its sparkling star, this tree sampler, opposite,
wraps all the recollections of Christmas into one glorious
package. Detailed with lovely shading and tiny seed beads,
it's the perfect project for early-bird crafters.

Eleventh-hour stitchers can enjoy the sampler with
quicker projects. Pick favorite motifs for perforated paper
ornaments that are finished in a flash with suede paper
backing. Or stitch the row of tree motifs into a pretty
band to skirt your holiday pie or casserole.

Project instructions begin on page 32.
Design: Ursula Michael. Photographs: Scott Little and Perry Struse

*D*rawing *from centuries-old samplers, these striking pieces team over-one stitching, traditional cross-stitches, and elegant bargello, worked in Florentine stitch. The framed piece,* opposite, *features majestic stag motifs, common on samplers from 1758 to 1826. Add an authentic feel by stitching it with overdyed thread. Repeat the bargello motif using standard floss to create a gift of beauty—a stunning vanity tray.*

Project instructions begin on page 35.
Design: Lauren Sauer for Forget-Me-Nots In Stitches. Photographs: Steve Struse and Perry Struse

Everyone knows the best treats are the homemade kind. And that's what makes this package—crafted in cross-stitch and cooked up in the kitchen—doubly sweet. Vivian's cookie box is an adaptation of a candy tin from the 1920s. Stitch the tin's original holly design, then paint and crackle a papier-mâché box to give it a rich patina. For last-minute project ideas, turn to pages 38–39.

Project instructions begin on page 38.
Design adaptation: Lynn Daugherty. Photographs: Marcia Cameron

Who can resist a blanket of fresh, pristine snow? For generations, snowsuited children have swished their outstretched limbs through the snow to form the most glorious angels. This frosty design, opposite, *catches the fun and the spirit of the moment in simple cross-stitches on pale blue linen. You can almost feel the powdery snow.*

Project instructions begin on page 40.
Design: Diana Thomas Studio. Photograph: Perry Struse

Christmas Tree Sampler

Anchor		DMC	
002	·	000	White
1049	☆	301	Mahogany
9046	○	321	True Christmas red
401	●	413	Pewter
370	✗	434	Chestnut
1045	−	436	Dark tan
1005	#	498	Dark Christmas red
228	▢	700	Medium Christmas green
239	╱	702	Light Christmas green
256	+	704	Chartreuse
361	∿	738	Light tan
043	♥	815	Garnet
306	◉	3820	Dark straw
891	◇	3822	Light straw
028	♡	3832	Raspberry

BACKSTITCH

002	╱	000 White – gingerbread people icing (2X)
1005	╱	498 Dark Christmas red – candy canes, mittens, ribbons, holly berries, gingerbread people icing (2X), mouths (1X)
228	╱	700 Medium Christmas green – lighting wire and holly leaves (2X)
358	╱	801 Coffee brown – bears, bells, birdhouse, drum, lights, stocking, and gingerbread people (1X), bell chain (2X)
382	╱	3371 Black-brown – bow on bells, teddy bear eyes and noses, and gingerbread people eyes (2X)
306	╱	3820 Dark straw – stars (2X)

MILL HILL BEADS

	◉	00128 Yellow seed beads – tree ornaments
	○	00479 White seed beads – gingerbread cookie detail, and center of red stars
	●	02014 Black seed beads – bear and gingerbread eyes and noses

Stitch count: 165 high x 140 wide

Finished design sizes:
14-count fabric – 11¾ x 10 inches
16-count fabric – 10⅓ x 8¾ inches
18-count fabric – 9⅛ x 7¾ inches

Christmas Tree Sampler

supplies
16×18" piece of 14-count antique white Aida cloth
Cotton embroidery floss
Mill Hill seed beads
Desired frame

stitches
Center and stitch the chart on the Aida cloth. Use three plies of floss to work the stitches over one square unless otherwise specified. Attach seed beads with two plies of matching floss. Press the stitched piece from the back. Frame as desired.

Christmas Tree Sampler

Sampler Mini Ornaments

The chart and key are on pages 32–33.

supplies

9×12" sheet of 14-count cream
   perforated paper
Cotton embroidery floss
9×12" sheet of card stock
9×12" sheet *each* of red and green
   suede paper
Newsprint or tissue paper
Spray adhesive for paper
Chenille needle

stitches

Cut the perforated paper into eighths to make eight 3×4½" rectangles. Center and stitch one motif (birdhouse, stocking, star, teddy bear, tree, gingerbread boy, gingerbread girl, and drum) from the Christmas Tree Sampler chart on each rectangle. Use two plies of floss to work the stitches over one square unless otherwise specified and omit the beads.

assembly

Cut the card stock in half, forming a 9×6" rectangle. Cut each sheet of suede paper in half in the same manner. (Reserve one suede-paper rectangle of each color for another purpose.) Protecting the work surface with newsprint, spray the back of each suede-paper rectangle with adhesive and adhere to one of the card-stock rectangles. Press to adhere.

Cut out each stitched motif one square beyond the stitching. When all of the ornaments are cut out, lay them facedown on a protected surface and spray with adhesive. Press the stocking, birdhouse, drum, and tree onto the green suede paper and the remaining motifs on the red suede paper. Cut out ⅛" beyond the perforated paper. For a hanger, use the chenille needle to thread floss that matches the suede-paper backing through the top of the ornament.

Christmas Tree Casserole Wrap

The chart and key are on pages 32–33.

supplies

13" length of 2"-wide 16-count
   green-and-white Aida-cloth
   banding
Cotton embroidery floss
⅜ yard of 45"-wide print fabric
Fusible interfacing
Matching sewing thread
1×2½" strip of Velcro

stitches

Center and stitch the row of trees from the Christmas Tree Sampler chart on the banding. Use two plies of floss to work the stitches over one square unless otherwise specified. Press the stitched banding from the back.

assembly

Trim the banding 1" beyond the stitched area on each end. From the print fabric, cut two 5×25" strips. Cut a 1¾×9" strip and two 2×25" strips of interfacing. All measurements include a ½" seam allowance.

Press the 5×25" fabric strips in half lengthwise. Position a 25" interfacing strip on the wrong side of each print fabric strip, aligning one long edge of the interfacing with the fold. Following the manufacturer's instructions, fuse the interfacing to the fabric strips and the 9" interfacing strip centered on the wrong side of the banding.

With right sides together, sew one short edge of each print fabric strip to an opposite short edge of the banding, aligning the banding with the interfacing on the fabric strips. Press the seam allowances away from the banding.

Sew together the remaining raw edges of each fabric strip with right sides facing. Trim the seams and clip the corners. Turn the fabric strips right side out. Press. Slipstitch the pressed edge of the fabric to the back of the banding. Center and edge-stitch the loop half of Velcro to the wrong side of one end of the casserole wrap and the hook half to the right side of the opposite end.

Bargello Tray
The chart and key are on pages 36–37.

supplies
12×15" piece of 28-count lambswool
   linen
Cotton embroidery floss
Desired frame with glass
4—½"-diameter stick-on rubber pads
2 brass window pulls
Short brass screws (optional)

stitches
Fold the fabric in half. On one half, work the Florentine and cross-stitch border portion of the O, Star of Wonder chart indicated by the dotted line. Turn the fabric upside down and stitch the same portion again, connecting the borders. Use two plies of floss to work the stitches over two threads of the fabric unless otherwise specified. Press the stitched piece from the back. Frame as desired, except omit a hanger and add a stick-on rubber pad to each corner. Attach a window pull to each end. (Depending on the thickness of the molding used for your frame, it may be necessary to purchase shorter screws than those that are included with the window pulls.)

O, Star of Wonder
The chart and key are on pages 36–37.

supplies
12" square of 32-count cream Sienna
   linen
Weeks Dyeworks overdyed floss
Frame

stitches
Center and stitch the chart on the fabric. Use two plies of floss to cross-stitch the stag and tree motifs. When using overdyed floss, complete each stitch before beginning the next. Use one ply of floss to work the star and lettering over one thread of fabric. Work the remaining stitches as specified in the key. Press the stitched piece from the back and frame as desired.

   Note: Not suitable for Aida cloth.

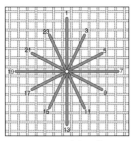

Diamond Eyelet

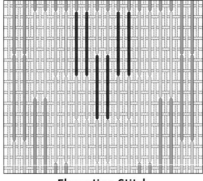

Florentine Stitch

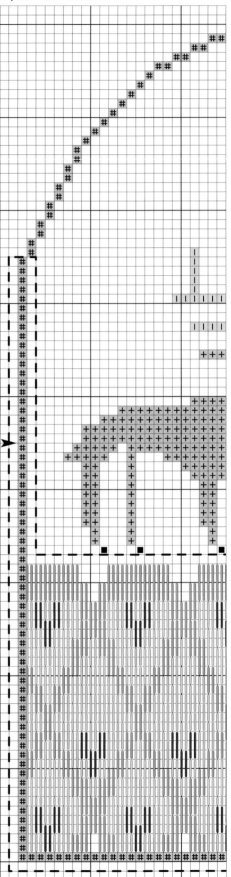

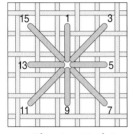

Algerian Eyelet

O, Star of Wonder

Anchor		DMC		Weeks Dye Works	
215	⬭	320	Pistachio	2156	Hunter
683	⊞	500	Blue-green	1279	Holly
127	⊠	823	Navy	1306	Navy
380	▲	838	Deep beige-brown	1269	Chestnut
379	✛	840	Medium beige-brown	1236	Mocha
382	■	3371	Black-brown	1304	Onyx
899	⊡	3782	Mocha	1151	Pebble
363	☆	3827	Golden brown	1224	Amber

ALGERIAN EYELET (1X)

127	✳	823	Navy – "e"	1306	Navy
363	✳	3827	Golden brown – star	1224	Amber

DIAMOND EYELET (1X)

363	✱	3827	Golden brown – star	1224	Amber

FLORENTINE STITCH (2X)

215	‖	320	Pistachio	2156	Hunter
1005	‖	498	Christmas red	2264	Garnet
683	‖	500	Blue-green	1279	Holly
363	‖	3827	Golden brown	1224	Amber

Stitch count: *90 high x 97 wide*
Finished design sizes:
32-count fabric – 5⅝ x 6 inches
28-count fabric – 6⅜ x 7 inches
36-count fabric – 5 x 5⅓ inches

Star of Wonder petite

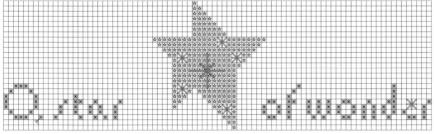

One Square = One thread

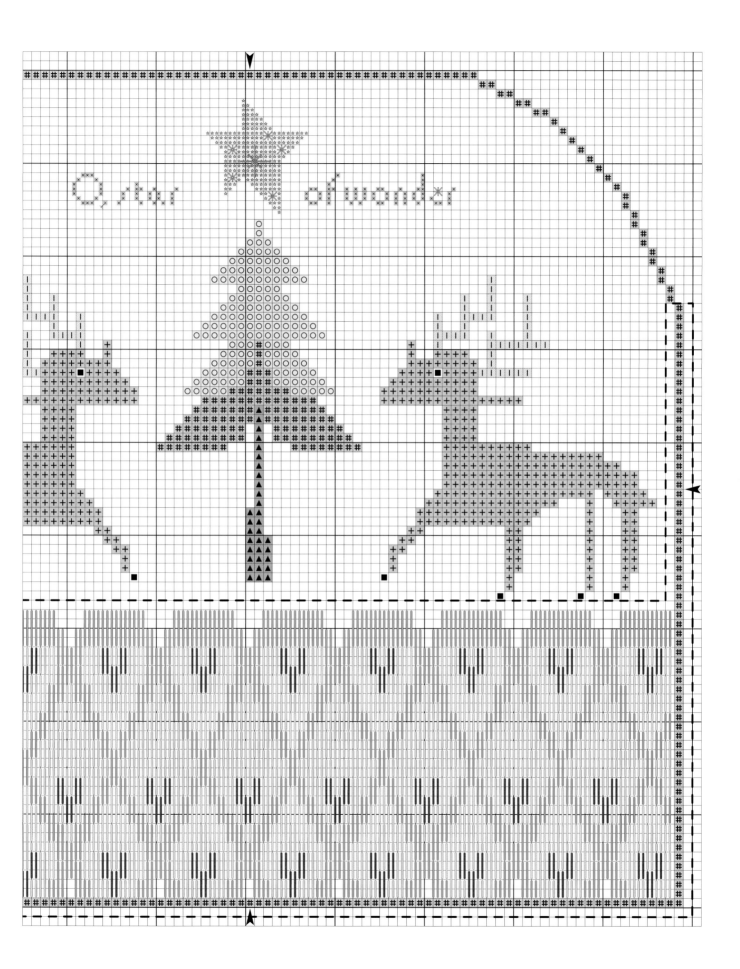

Antique Candy Tin

supplies

12" square of 28-count country French latte linen
Cotton embroidery floss
Graph paper
8"-diameter papier-mâché box with picture frame insert
Pencil and ruler
Christmas red, medium green, light green, and dark blue acrylic paints
Sponge brush
½" flat paintbrushes
¾"-diameter snowflake rubber stamp
Gold stamp pad
Gold embossing powder
Embossing or other heating tool
Aleene's Mosaic Crackle Medium Steps 1 and 2
8"-diameter circle of thick batting
Spray adhesive
Fabric tape
8"-diameter circle of red felt

Stitches

Chart the desired label using the alphabet, *opposite*. Using the chart as a guide for positioning the label, center and stitch the chart and label on the linen. Use three plies of floss to work the stitches over two threads of the fabric

unless otherwise specified. Press the stitched piece from the back.

assembly

Remove the lid from the box and set it aside. With the sponge brush, paint the sides of the box bottom medium green; allow the paint to dry. If desired, use a pencil and ruler to mark vertical lines, about 2½" apart all the way around the box. Use the ½" flat brush to paint a light green stripe from top to bottom every 2½". Allow the stripes to dry.

With pencil and ruler, draw a line horizontally around the box, 1¼" from the bottom. Randomly rubber-stamp snowflakes on about one-fourth of the painted portion of the box above the horizontal line. While the ink is wet, sprinkle embossing powder on the snowflakes, and tap off the excess. Use the embossing tool or hair dryer to gently heat the design until the powder melts. Repeat around the box.

Paint the area below the drawn line and the bottom of the box dark blue; set aside to dry.

Remove the inner cardboard circle from the box lid and set it aside. Following the manufacturer's directions, mix red paint with the Step 1 crackle medium. Apply to the outer portion

of the box lid. Then follow the directions for Step 2 and allow to dry.

Center the cardboard insert from the lid on the back of stitched piece and draw around it. Cut out the stitched piece ½" beyond the drawn line. Mount the batting circle on the cardboard insert using spray adhesive. Cover the batting with the stitched piece. Wrap the excess to the back and secure with tape. Tape the cardboard insert inside the lid of the box. Mount the felt circle to the back of the cardboard insert with spray adhesive.

Bag Label

supplies

6" square 14-count China pearl Aida cloth
Dark Christmas red (DMC 498) cotton embroidery floss
Graph paper
Sewing thread to match fabric

stitches

Chart the desired wording using the Antique Candy Tin alphabet, *opposite*. Center and stich your chart on the fabric. Use two plies of red floss to work the stitches over one square. Press the stitched piece from the back. Machine-sew around the stitches seven squares beyond the cross-stitches. Trim away excess fabric four squares beyond the machine stitches. Fringe the edges by removing threads between the cut edge and the stitches.

Antique Candy Tin

Anchor		DMC	
9046	♡	321	True Christmas red
1005	●	498	Dark Christmas red
046	+	666	Red
047	□	817	Coral
1044	#	895	Hunter green
266	△	3347	Medium yellow-green
862	∕	3348	Light yellow-green
1098	✕	3801	Watermelon

BACKSTITCH (1X)

1044	╱	895	Hunter green – lettering
382	╱	3371	Black-brown – all other stitches

FRENCH KNOT (1X wrapped twice)

002	○	000	White – holly berries

Stitch count: 60 high x 48 wide

Finished design sizes:
28-count fabric – 4¼ x 3½ inches
32-count fabric – 3¾ x 3 inches
36-count fabric – 3⅓ x 2⅔ inches

Antique Candy Tin

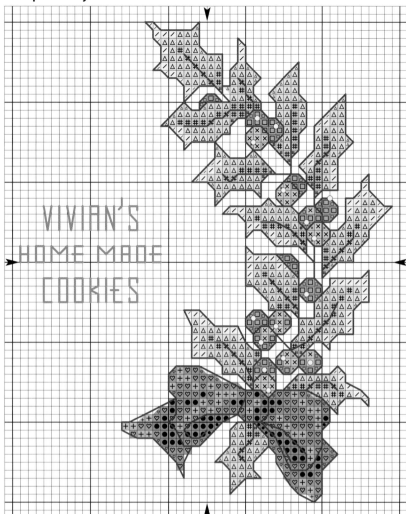

Holly Paperweight

supplies
8" square 18-count silver-and-white Aida cloth
Cotton embroidery floss
2¾×1⅛" rectangular beaded glass paperweight

stitches
Center and stitch the holly motif from the Antique Candy Tin chart on the Aida cloth. Use two plies of floss to work the stitches over one square of fabric unless otherwise specified. Work the French knots using one ply wrapped once. Press the stitched piece from the back. Mount in the paperweight following the manufacturer's instructions.

Antique Candy Tin Alphabet

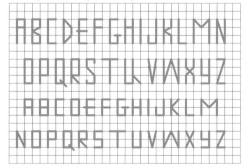

Snow Angels

supplies

15" square of 28-count Monet blue linen
Cotton embroidery floss
13½"-diameter crown plate frame
150-grit sandpaper
Medium blue and pearl white
  acrylic paints
Small flat paintbrushes
Crackling medium

stitches

Center and stitch the chart on the fabric. Use three plies of floss to work the stitches over two threads of the fabric unless otherwise specified. Press the stitched piece from the back.

assembly

To finish the frame, lightly sand all surfaces. Apply an even coat of medium blue paint. Allow the paint to dry. Following the manufacturer's instructions, apply and crackle the pearl white paint over the blue. Allow to dry thoroughly.

  Mount the stitched piece in the frame following manufacturer's instructions.

Snow Angels

Anchor		DMC	
002	•	000	White
403	■	310	Black
979	▲	312	Light navy
146	⊕	322	Pale navy
150	⋈	336	Medium navy
235	✳	414	Steel
398	◲	415	Pearl gray
370	✪	434	Chestnut
1045	✖	436	Tan
683	★	500	Blue-green
046	⊠	666	Red
305	✳	725	True topaz
295	⊟	726	Light topaz
159	−	775	Light baby blue
358	✚	801	Coffee brown
045	▶	814	Garnet
228	⊞	910	True emerald
205	▽	912	Light emerald
882	∧	945	Dark ivory
1010	▢	951	Medium ivory
206	⋮	955	Nile green
292	Ⅰ	3078	Lemon
144	○	3325	Medium baby blue
035	◉	3705	Dark watermelon
033	#	3706	Medium watermelon
031	◎	3708	Light watermelon
140	▯	3755	Dark baby blue
868	╱	3779	Terra-cotta
306	⊠	3820	Straw

BACKSTITCH (1X)

002	╱	000	White – girl's hat detail (2X)
235	╱	414	Steel – girl's hat detail (2X)
205	╱	912	Light emerald – boy's scarf fringe (2X)
206	╱	955	Nile green – boy's scarf stripes (2X)
382	╱	3371	Black-brown – all other stitches (1X)
035	╱	3705	Dark watermelon – mouths (1X)
140	╱	3755	Dark baby blue – snow lines near feet (2X)

ALGERIAN EYELET

140	✳	3755	Dark baby blue – large snowflakes (1X)

FRENCH KNOT

002	○	000	White – small snowflakes on children and letters (1X wrapped twice)
205	●	912	Light emerald – scarf fringe (2X wrapped once)
140	●	3755	Dark baby blue – small snowflakes in background (1X wrapped twice)

Stitch count: *126 high x 128 wide*
Finished design sizes:
28-count fabric – 9 x 9⅛ inches
32-count fabric – 7⅞ x 8 inches
36-count fabric – 7 x 7⅛ inches

Snow Angels

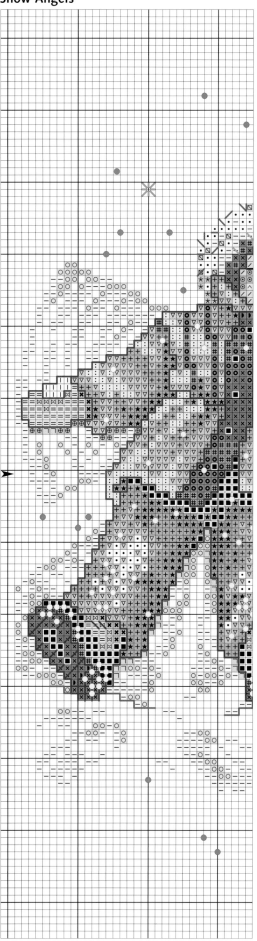

House Full

# of Santa

The magic of Santa fills our hearts and homes every December. Yet somehow, as cross-stitchers and collectors, we never seem to get our fill! Thanks to creative designers, this collection is packed with new looks and delightful ways to spread the jolly old elf's holiday cheer all through the house.

*T*uck *these celestial Santas into a tabletop display*, slip them over the branches on your Christmas tree, or give them as gifts. One ornament is finished pillow-style and trimmed in golden cording. The perforated paper version, in front, gets a double backing of stiff felt for a fast, sturdy finish. Remember to add the star charm at the tip of his cap!

Project instructions begin on page 52.
Design: Ursula Michael. Photograph: Steve Struse

If you've a penchant for folk art, you'll love this interpretation of St. Nick, opposite. He wears the customary coat of an old-world figure, but that's where tradition ends and country takes over. Look at the oversized pockets and his birdhouse staff! A real treat to stitch on rugged 11-count Aida, the piece is framed in cross-stitch gingham, then set into a pillow with quilt sashing and buttons in each corner.

Project instructions begin on page 54.
Design: Robin Kingsley. Photograph: Scott Little

A trio of portraits showcases all the detail
and character true to a 20th-century Santa. For the decorative
bell pull, join the "snapshots" with faux ribbon on 30-count
linen, opposite. Enlarge your favorite to 26-count fabric and
frame it. For ornaments, work the images on navy blue
Aida cloth and eliminate the background.

Project instructions begin on page 56.
Design: Carol Emmer. Photographs: Scott Little, Marcia Cameron, and Perry Struse

Heads up, forward, march!

Eight traditional Santas take a spin on this miniature tree skirt, opposite. Filled with Christmas potential, the same cavalcade adapts easily for a festive wreath decoration. Stitched individually, backed, and finished with an oval base, they turn into freestanding dolls to decorate your holiday house. Or work your favorite Santa on perforated paper to make a delightful gift add-on, ornament, or plant poke.

Project instructions begin on page 59.
Design: Robin Clark. Photographs: Marcia Cameron and Perry Struse

There's no mistaking this full-figured fellow. Dressed in red, white, and blue, he's as American as apple pie. What's more, he's as easy as pie to finish! Stitched on a prefinished towel, this jolly old elf brings holiday cheer to the kitchen or guest bath.

Project instructions begin opposite.
Design: Ursula Michael. Photograph: Steve Struse

Santa Towel

supplies

Purchased 15×25" white huck towel with a 4¼×5¾" 14-count Aida-cloth insert
Cotton embroidery floss

stitches

Center and stitch the chart on the Aida-cloth towel insert. Use three plies of floss to work the stitches over one square unless otherwise specified. Press the finished towel from the back.

Santa Towel

Anchor		DMC	
926	–		Ecru
002	•	000	White
403	■	310	Black
400	+	317	Pewter
9046	×	321	True Christmas red
1005	#	498	Dark Christmas red
391	✳	644	Beige-gray
302	I	743	Yellow
122	▲	792	Dark cornflower blue
176	╱	793	Medium cornflower blue
045	◪	814	Garnet
1012	╲	948	Peach
382	✚	3371	Black-brown
868	◯	3779	Terra-cotta

BACKSTITCH (1X)

403	╱	310 Black – boots and belt
382	╱	3371 Black-brown – all other stitches

Stitch count: 71 high x 43 wide

Finished design sizes:
14-count fabric – 5 x 3 inches
16-count fabric – 4⅜ x 2⅔ inches
18-count fabric – 4 x 2⅓ inches

Santa Towel

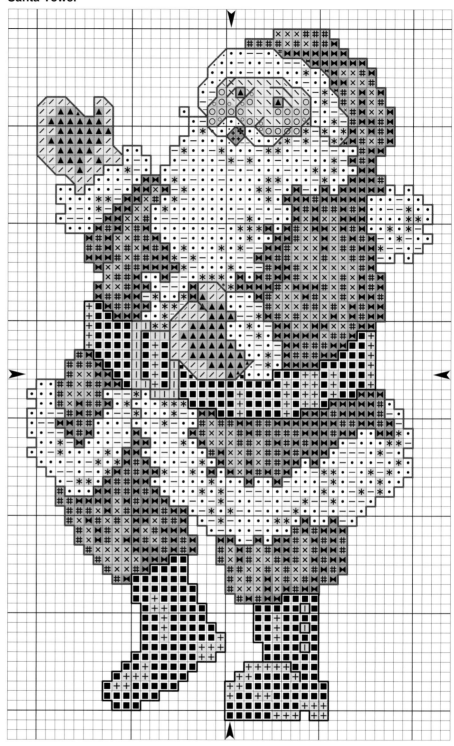

assembly

Peel the protective paper from the mounting board. Center the foam side on the back of the stitched piece and press to stick. Trim the excess fabric ⅜" beyond the edge of the board. Fold the edge of the fabric to the back and glue in place.

Position and glue the cord around the edge of the ornament, overlapping the cord and forming a loop at the top center. Trim the excess cord and glue the ends to the ornament back. Glue the felt to the back of the ornament.

Santa Moon Perforated Paper Ornament

supplies

6" square of 14-count cream perforated paper
Cotton embroidery floss
5" square each of white and red stiffened felt
Crafts glue
¾"-tall star brass charm
Kreinik gold (002C) cord or other fine cord

stitches

Center and stitch the chart on the perforated paper, eliminating the star, tie, and bow. Use two plies of floss to work the stitches unless otherwise specified.

assembly

Trim the stitched piece one square beyond the stitched area of the design. Center the stitched piece on the white felt and glue in place. Trim away the excess white felt ⅛" beyond the perforated paper. Center and glue the white felt shape on the red felt. Trim the excess red felt ⅛" beyond the white felt.

Referring to the photograph, *above,* use gold cord to attach the star charm.

Santa Moon Fabric Ornament

supplies

9" square piece of 28-count sky blue linen
Cotton embroidery floss
Kreinik gold (002) blending filament
5"-diameter circle of self-stick mounting board with foam
5"-diameter circle of light blue felt
½ yard of ¼"-diameter metallic gold twisted cord
Crafts glue

stitches

Center and stitch the chart on the linen. Use three plies of floss to work the stitches over two threads of the fabric unless otherwise specified. Press the stitched piece from the back.

Santa Moon Ornament

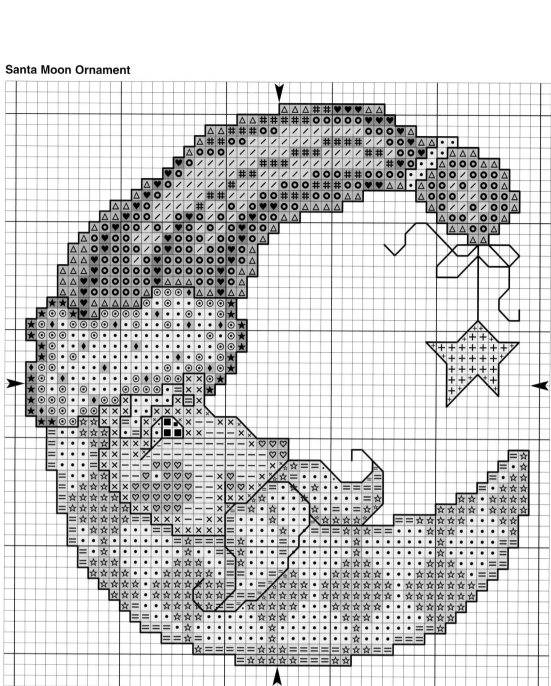

Anchor		DMC	
1006	△	304	Christmas red
403	■	310	Black
013	◉	349	Dark coral
010	╱	351	Light coral
855	☆	612	Drab brown
391	＝	644	Light beige-gray
045	♥	814	Dark garnet
1005	#	816	Light garnet
390	•	822	Pale beige-gray
882	✕	945	Dark ivory
1010	─	951	Medium ivory
903	◎	3032	Medium mocha
1013	♡	3778	Terra-cotta
1050	◆	3781	Dark mocha
1088	★	3790	Deep beige-gray

Anchor		DMC	
BLENDED NEEDLE			
305	✚	3821	Straw (2X) and 002 Kreinik Gold blending filament (1X)
BACKSTITCH			
382	╱	3371	Black-brown – tie and bow on star (2X), all other stitches (1X)

Stitch count: *52 high x 48 wide*
Finished design sizes:
14-count fabric – 3¾ x 3⅜ inches
16-count fabric – 3¼ x 3 inches
18-count fabric – 2⅞ x 2⅔ inches

Folk Art Santa

supplies

14×18" piece of 11-count beige
    Aida cloth
⅛ yard of 45"-wide red cotton fabric
½ yard of 45"-wide blue cotton fabric
1⅝ yards of ¼"-diameter cording
12½×15¼" piece of fusible fleece
Polyester fiberfill
1"-tall birdhouse, Christmas tree, star,
    and mitten buttons

stitches

Center and stitch the design from the chart on the fabric. Use three plies of floss to work the cross-stitches over one square of fabric unless otherwise specified.

assembly

Centering the design, trim the stitched piece to a 12½×9¾" rectangle. From the red fabric, cut two 2×12½" side sashing strips and two 2×9¾" strips for the top and bottom sashing. From the blue fabric, cut a 12¾×15½" back and four 2×2" squares for corners. Also from the blue fabric, cut and join enough 1⅜"-wide strips to make to make a 60"-long piping strip.

With raw edges even, sew one side sashing strip to each side of the stitched piece using ¼" seams. Press the seams toward the sashing. Sew corner squares to ends of top and bottom sashing strips. Sew top and bottom sashing strips to the stitched piece. Press the seams toward the sashing.

Fuse the fleece to the back of the pieced pillow front following the manufacturer's instructions.

Center the cording lengthwise on the wrong side of the piping strip. Fold the fabric over the cording, with the long edges together. Using a zipper foot, sew close to the cording through all layers. Sew the piping around the perimeter of the pillow front with raw edges even.

Sew the pillow front and back together with right sides facing and raw edges even, leaving an opening for turning. Clip the corners and turn right side out. Press the pillow carefully. Stuff firmly with polyester fiberfill. Slip-stitch the opening closed.

Sew the corresponding buttons on corner squares.

Folk Art Santa

Anchor		DMC	
926	⊡		Ecru
371	✖	433	Dark chestnut
1046	⊕	435	Light chestnut
885	◯	677	Pale old gold
891	✳	729	Medium old gold
1022	◲	760	Salmon
360	◆	898	Dark coffee brown
897	▲	902	Garnet
1034	✕	931	Medium antique blue
921	⊞	932	True antique blue
381	■	938	Deep coffee brown
882	⊟	945	Ivory
266	➕	3347	Medium yellow-green
862	◿	3348	Light yellow-green
1031	△	3753	Pale antique blue
1008	◹	3773	Rose-beige
1015	➕	3777	Deep terra-cotta
339	✪	3830	Terra-cotta

BACKSTITCH (1X)
| 897 | ╱ | 902 | Garnet – border |
| 382 | ╱ | 3371 | Black-brown – all other stitches |

FRENCH KNOT
| 382 | ● | 3371 | Black-brown – nails on birdhouse platform |

Stitch count: 130 high x 98 wide
Finished design sizes:
11-count fabric – 11¾ x 9 inches
14-count fabric – 9¼ x 7 inches
16-count fabric – 8⅛ x 6⅛ inches

Anchor		DMC
979	☒	312 Navy
9046	◫	321 True Christmas red
009	▯	352 Coral
868	▽	353 Dark peach
817	✚	469 Dark avocado
267	◉	470 Medium avocado
265	▯▯	471 Light avocado
1005	▦	498 Dark Christmas red
889	★	610 Deep drab brown
898	▸	611 Dark drab brown
855	⋒	612 Medium drab brown
393	◇	640 Dark beige-gray
392	⊞	642 Medium beige-gray
391	⌐	644 Light beige-gray
046	△	666 Red
874	⑀	676 Light old gold
885	◥	677 Pale old gold
305	✛	725 True topaz
295	◿	726 Light topaz
891	◆	729 Medium old gold
9575	⋈	758 Light terra-cotta
1022	♡	760 True salmon
309	▲	781 Dark topaz
308	◎	782 Medium topaz
307	⊡	783 Christmas gold
390	⁄	822 Pale beige-gray
906	✺	829 Bronze
897	▼	902 Garnet
1034	◆	931 Medium antique blue

Framed Santa

supplies
10" square of 26-count ivory linen
Cotton embroidery floss
Kreinik blending filament
Desired mat and frame

stitches
Center and stitch the desired Bell Pull
Santa chart (we used Santa A) on the
fabric, omitting the rectangles at the top
and bottom. Use three plies of floss to
work the stitches over two threads of
fabric. Press the stitched piece from the
back. Frame as desired.

Bell Pull Santa A

Anchor		DMC	
921	⊛	932	True antique blue
1012	□	948	Light peach
360	■	3031	Deep mocha
883	✳	3064	Light cocoa
1023	⊡	3712	Medium salmon
1020	✶	3713	Pale salmon
1096	◰	3752	Light antique blue
1009	⊟	3770	True ivory
1007	◀	3772	Dark cocoa
1050	▣	3781	Dark mocha
1098	⊟	3801	Watermelon
002	⊡	3865	Winter white

BLENDED NEEDLE

891	✵	729 Medium old gold (1x) and 002 Kreinik gold blending filament (1X)

BACKSTITCH

5975	╱	356 Medium terra-cotta – Santas' and dolls' faces
817	╱	469 Dark avocado – top of Santa's package
393	╱	640 Dark beige-gray – top and bottom of Santa's fur
046	╱	666 Red – top of doll bonnet, bottom of doll bow, horse bridle
308	╱	782 Medium topaz – bottom of Santa's package
1034	╱	931 Medium antique blue – dolls' eyes
360	╱	3031 Deep mocha – all remaining stitches
	╱	002 Kreinik gold #4 very fine braid – border

STRAIGHT STITCH

002	╱	3865 Winter white – eyebrows
	╱	002 Kreinik gold #4 very fine braid – border

FRENCH KNOT

360	●	3031 Deep mocha – horse's eye and mane (1X wrapped once)

MILL HILL BEADS

	◎	00557 Gold seed bead

Stitch count: *208 high x 56 wide*

Finished design sizes:
30-count fabric – 13⅞ x 3¾ inches
28-count fabric – 14⅞ x 4 inches
32-count fabric – 13 x 3½ inches

Bell Pull Santas B and C

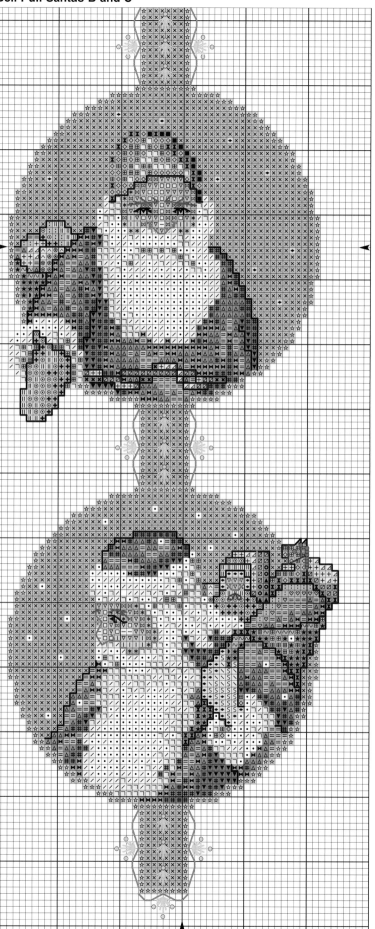

Bell Santa Pull

The charts and key are on pages 56–57.

supplies

10×20" piece of 30-count clay linen
Cotton embroidery floss
Kreinik #4 very fine braid
Kreinik blending filament
Mill Hill seed beads
5¾×19" piece of fleece
5¾×19" piece of beige cotton fabric
Matching sewing thread
38" of ⅛"-diameter metallic gold
   twisted cord
5½" bell pull hardware

stitches

Stitch the Bell Pull Santas B and C chart
on the linen, centering Santa B. Use two
plies of floss to work the stitches over
two threads of the fabric unless otherwise
specified. Attach the seed beads using two
plies of matching floss. Then stitch Bell
Pull Santa A above Santa B. Press the
stitched piece from the back.

assembly

Centering the design, trim the fabric to
measure 5¾×19". (Measurements include
¼" seam allowances unless otherwise
specified.) Position the fleece on the
back of the stitched piece and baste
along the long edges. With right sides

together, sew the beige fabric to the
stitched piece along the long edges.
Trim the seams, turn right side out, and
press. Zigzag-stitch the top and bottom
edges. Cut the metallic gold cord in half
and hand-sew to the long edges of the
bell pull.

Press the top and bottom edges of
the bell pull under ½". Insert the top and
bottom of the bell pull through the
corresponding hardware pieces,
overlapping the back about 2". Slip-stitch
the folded edge to the back.

Santa Ornaments

The charts and key are on pages 56–57.

supplies

For each ornament
10" square of 14-count navy Aida cloth
Cotton embroidery floss
Kreinik blending filament
5¾" circle of medium-weight cardboard
5¾" circle of fleece
Spray adhesive
5¾" circle of navy felt
½ yard of ⅛"-diameter metallic gold
   twisted cord

stitches

Center and stitch one Santa motif on the
Aida cloth, omitting the rectangles at the
top and bottom. Use three plies of floss
to work the stitches over two threads of
the fabric unless otherwise specified. If
desired, substitute winter white (DMC
3865) for the stars on Santa B. Press the
stitched piece from the back.

assembly

Attach the fleece circle to the
cardboard circle with spray adhesive.
Center the stitched piece on the fleece.
Trim the excess fabric ⅜" beyond the
edge of the board. Fold the edge of the
fabric to the back and glue in place.

Position and glue the cord around
the edge of the ornament,
overlapping the cord and forming a
loop at the top center. Trim the
excess cord and glue the ends to the
ornament back. Glue the felt to the
back of the ornament.

Santas on Parade Mini Tree Skirt

The chart and key are on pages 60–61.

supplies

16" square of 26-count birch
   Heatherfield fabric
Cotton embroidery floss
14" square of polyester fleece
14" square of light gray broadcloth
Sewing thread to match fabrics
1⅛ yards ½"-wide flat lace trim

stitches

Center and stitch the chart on the fabric.
Use three plies of floss to work the
cross-stitches over two threads of fabric.
Work backstitches and French knots as
specified in the key. Press the stitched
piece from the back.

assembly

Center the fleece on the back of the
stitched piece. Use one ply of dark floss
to baste through both layers along the
dotted lines indicated on the chart. With
right sides together, machine-sew the
stitched piece to the broadcloth,
stitching around the inner circle and the
outer circle on the basted lines. Trim the
seam allowance to ¼" on the outer edge.
Cut through all layers along the basted
straight line. Trim the inner circle seam
allowance to ¼" and clip curves. Press
the straight edges under ⅛". Turn the
tree skirt right side and press. Slipstitch
the straight edges of the stitched piece
and the lining together on each side.
Slip-stitch lace to the outer edge of the
tree skirt.

Santas on Parade Ornaments

The chart and key are on pages 60–61.

supplies

For each ornament
4" square of 14-count cream perforated
   paper
Cotton embroidery floss
6" square of green stiffened felt
Spray adhesive
Wooden skewer

Center and fuse the interfacing to the back of the stitchery following the manufacturer's instructions. Center the body pattern over the stitchery and use the erasable fabric marker to draw the shape onto the stitched piece. Cut out ½" beyond the drawn line.

Use the stitched piece as a pattern to cut a matching back from the plaid fabric. Also, cut a 1½×12" bias piping strip from the plaid fabric.

Center the cording lengthwise on the wrong side of the piping strip. Fold the fabric around the cording with the long edges together. Use a zipper foot to sew through both layers close to the cording. Baste the piping around the side and top edges of the doll front with the raw edges even.

With right sides together and using the zipper foot, sew the doll front to the back along the basting lines, leaving the bottom edge open. Trim the seams, clip the curves, and turn right side out.

Trace the base pattern on the cardboard and cut out. Draw around the cardboard oval on the plaid fabric. Cut out ½" beyond the traced line. Center and glue the cardboard to the back of the plaid fabric. Fold the raw edges to the back and glue. Let the glue dry.

Stuff the body firmly with fiberfill. Fold the bottom edge of the body under ½". Hand-stitch the base to the bottom of the body.

stitches

Center and stitch the desired Santa on the paper. Use three plies of floss to work the cross-stitches over one square of paper. Work the backstitches and French knots as specified in the key. Trim the stitched piece one square beyond the stitching. Mount it on felt with spray adhesive. Trim ⅛" beyond the paper. Gently push the skewer between the perforated paper and the felt.

Santas on Parade Dolls

supplies

For each doll

10" square of 10-count cream Tula fabric
Cotton embroidery floss
2—6" squares of tracing paper
6" square of fusible interfacing
Erasable fabric marker
¼ yard of coordinating plaid fabric
Matching sewing thread
⅜ yard of ⅛"-diameter cording
3×5" rectangle of medium-weight
    cardboard
Crafts glue
Polyester fiberfill

stitches

Center and stitch any Santa from the chart on one square of fabric. Use four plies of floss to work the stitches over one square unless otherwise specified. Press the finished stitchery facedown.

assembly

Fold each tracing paper square in half, and trace the body and base patterns, *page 60;* cut out on the traced lines and unfold each pattern.

Santas on Parade

Anchor		DMC	
002	·	000	White
897	♥	221	Shell pink
1025	⊠	347	Salmon
217	☆	367	Medium pistachio
1044	✳	500	Blue-green
860	▣	522	Dark olive drab
858	☰	524	Light olive drab
885	╱	677	Old gold
9575	▮	758	Terra-cotta
045	⊙	814	Garnet
683	●	890	Deep pistachio
1035	★	930	Dark antique blue
1034	⊕	931	Medium antique blue
921	☐	932	True antique blue
862	◆	934	Deep pine green
861	▦	935	Dark pine green
4146	△	950	Rose-beige
360	▲	3031	Deep mocha
903	◉	3032	Medium mocha
391	⋮	3033	Pale mocha
887	○	3045	Dark yellow-beige
886	△	3046	Medium yellow-beige
382	■	3371	Black-brown
1050	▶	3781	Dark mocha
899	◺	3782	Light mocha

Anchor		DMC	
BACKSTITCH			
897	╱	221	Shell pink – stripes on coat (2X)
861	╱	935	Dark pine green – stripes on pack (2X)
382	╱	3371	Black-brown – all other stitches (1X)
FRENCH KNOT			
382	●	3371	Black-brown – eyes (1X wrapped once)
382	●	3371	Black-brown – jingle bells of Santas 6 and 7 (1X wrapped twice)

Stitch count: 119 high x 119 wide

Finished design sizes:
25-count fabric – 9½ x 9½ inches
26-count fabric – 9⅛ x 9⅛ inches
28-count fabric – 8½ x 8½ inches

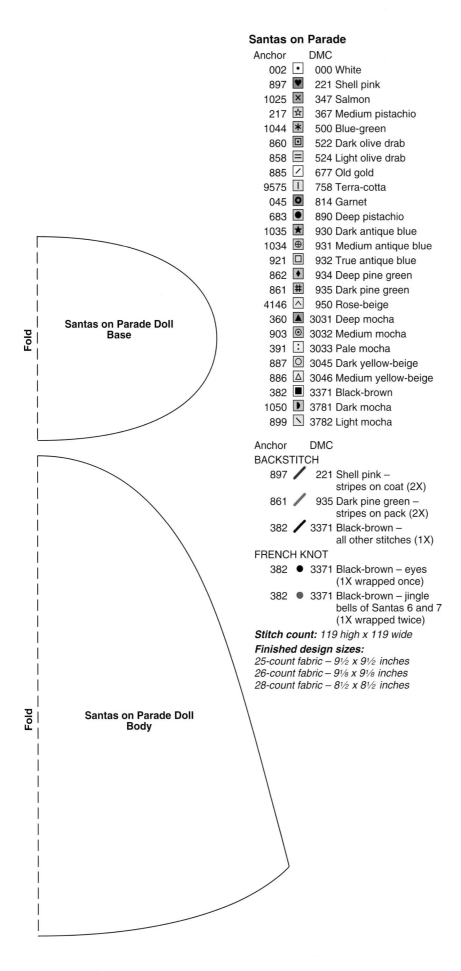

Fold

Santas on Parade Doll Base

Fold

Santas on Parade Doll Body

Santas on Parade

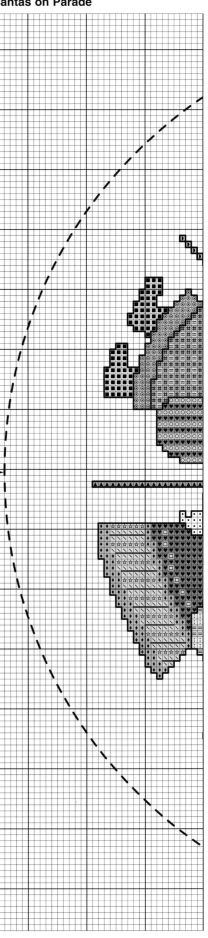

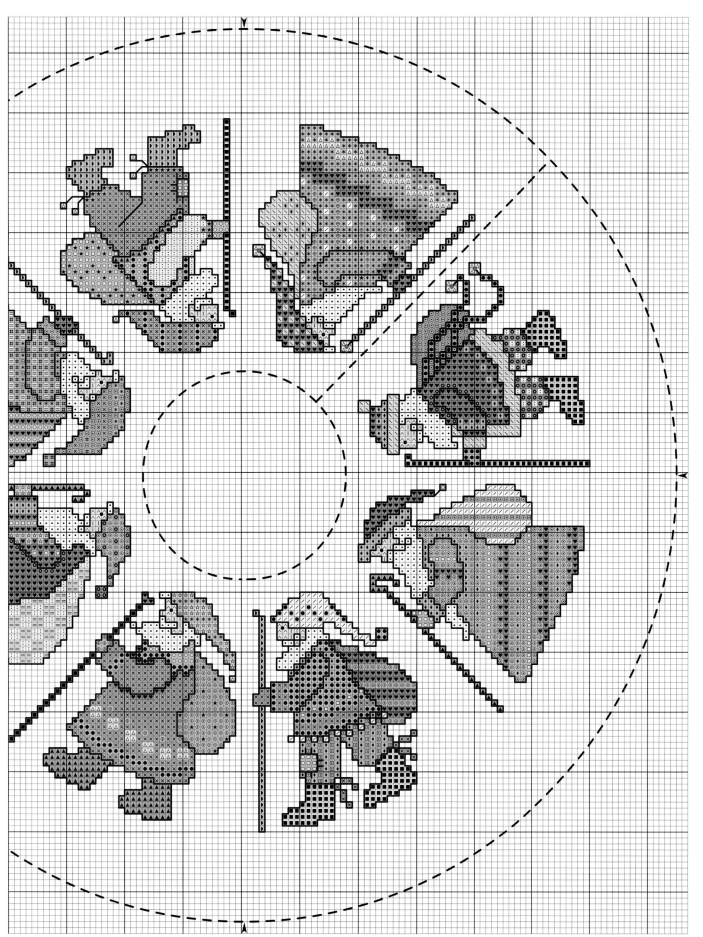

Stitched

for Giving

Christmas is the time

for giving the most carefully chosen gifts. To imaginative cross-stitchers, this means pulling out the needle and thread and creating the best ones right at their fingertips. Made by hand and with plenty of love, this delightful selection includes a wealth of ideas for both children and adults. Watch for shortcut ideas on the pages, too, then let them inspire your own heartfelt presents.

Santa and his friends make dressing for winter child's play. Stitched on prefinished Aida cloth shapes (two hearts and a circle), their cheery faces turn a toddler's frown around when patched to scarves, mittens, hats, and gloves. For a permanent fix, baste the shapes to the items. For easy removal, attach them with hook-and-loop fastening tape.

Project instructions begin on page 78.
Design: Barbara Sestok. Photograph: Marcia Cameron

'Tis the season for glitter, holiday flair, and everything ornamental. These accessories are all that—and more. Dainty French knots, metallic threads, and shaded bands of trees and holly leaves dress this handbag in tapestrylike elegance, opposite. *Worked on red Aida cloth, the handbag is designed as two pieces, so you can combine the embellished flap with brocade, wool, or velvet, for the body of the bag. For the brooch, use just a portion of the design. The floss colors remain the same as the handbag's, but the background switches to a heavenly blue.*

Project instructions begin on page 70.
Design: Hollis Minor for It's Polite to Point. Photographs: Steve Struse

Ring in the holidays and the new year royally *with glimmering bell tokens. The needle case in the foreground features a princess front sewn to a prince back. To use it, just give the emery "clapper" a pull to reveal a felt flap for easy needle storage. For quicker gifts, stitch the figures individually in another colorway and finish them as tree ornaments.*

Project instructions begin on page 72.
Design: Patricia Andrle. Photograph: Scott Little

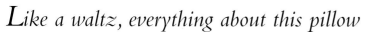

Like a waltz, everything about this pillow

flows with grace and beauty. From its cross-stitched blushing rose and lacy Hardanger frame to the soft green background lined in pink sateen, the design moves in a gentle harmony of color and embroidery. An exquisite gift for someone special, it's just as elegant worked on a smaller scale. The flower, used alone, puts a rosy bloom on a prefinished eyeglasses case.

Project instructions begin on page 74.
Design: Julia Lucas. Photographs: Scott Little and Marcia Cameron

*T*hrill your best crafting pals with this journal, then make one
to match for yourself! It's a wonderful way to preserve and share all the things you've
accomplished over the years. Sporting a traditional sampler design, the journal cover is fabric
bound and tied with ribbon to keep the information and photos safe inside. Special touches
of Florentine stitch, double cross-stitch stars, and eyelets punctuate the design.

Project instructions begin on page 76.
Design: Kandace Thomas. Photograph: Scott Little

*A*ll a child's dreams of Christmas joy come true
in this toyland sampler, opposite. Stitch and frame the entire piece for
a little one's room. Add bits and pieces of the design to
garments that the child can enjoy throughout the year. There
are enough creative ideas in this design to keep you in stitches
for all sorts of gift-giving occasions. Try the row of hearts across
a prefinished bib. Or turn to page 80 for an easy addition to
ready-made overalls or other garments.

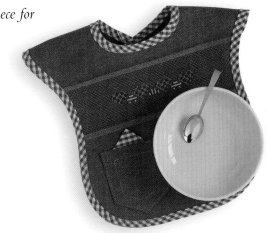

Project instructions begin on page 79.
Design: Robin Kingsley. Photographs: Scott Little and Marcia Cameron

Holiday Evening Bag

supplies
10×14" piece of 14-count Christmas red
   Aida cloth
Cotton embroidery floss
Metallic embroidery floss
10×12" piece of 14-count Christmas red
   Aida cloth or other fabric
10×20" piece of fusible fleece
10×20" piece of lining fabric
2½" of ⅛"-diameter red-and-gold
   twisted cord
1⅝ yard of ¼"-diameter red-and-gold
   twisted cord
Red sewing thread; crafts glue

stitches
Center and stitch the design from the
chart onto the 10×14" piece of Aida cloth.
Use three plies of floss to work the
cross-stitches over one square of fabric
unless otherwise specified. Work the
remaining stitches as specified in the key.
Press the stitched piece from the back.

Holiday Evening Bag

Anchor		DMC
683	■	500 Blue-green
874	•	676 Light old gold
891	−	729 Medium old gold
133	●	796 Royal blue
137	+	798 Delft blue
228	×	910 Emerald
	╱	5282 Metallic gold
	◎	5283 Metallic silver

BACKSTITCH (1X)

683	╱	500 Blue-green
228	╱	910 Emerald

FRENCH KNOT (1X wrapped twice)

9046	●	321 Christmas red
133	●	796 Royal blue
043	●	815 Garnet
	○	5282 Metallic gold
	○	5283 Metallic silver

Evening Bag Flap stitch count:
61 high x 126 wide

Evening Bag Flap finished design sizes:
14-count fabric – 4⅜ x 9 inches
16-count fabric – 3⅞ x 7⅞ inches
18-count fabric – 3⅜ x 7 inches

Holiday Evening Bag

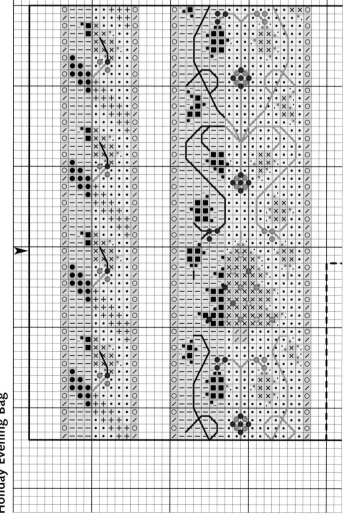

assembly

All seam allowances are ½" unless otherwise specified. Trim away excess fabric on the stitched piece ¾" beyond the stitching on the straight-side and top edges and ½" beyond the shaped bottom edge. With right sides together, sew the top edge of the stitched piece to one 10" edge of the unstitched Aida cloth.

Use the Aida cloth piece as a pattern to cut one piece from fleece and one from lining fabric. Fuse the fleece to the back of the Aida cloth following manufacturer's directions.

Fold the ⅛"-diameter cord in half to form a button loop. With raw edges even, center it on the stitched flap. Layer the Aida cloth piece and the lining, right sides together. Sew all the way around, leaving an opening for turning. Trim corners and clip curves. Turn right side out and press. Slipstitch the opening closed. With lining sides together, fold the plain Aida up 5¼" and slipstitch the sides of the bag together.

Apply glue to the ends of the ¼"-diameter cord; let dry. Tucking the glued ends between the stitches at the bottom edges of the bag, slipstitch one end of the cord to each side of the bag. Sew the button under the button loop.

Holiday Brooch

supplies

8×4" piece of 28-count antique blue linen
Cotton embroidery floss
Metallic embroidery floss
Erasable marker
Tracing paper
6×3" piece of polyester fleece
6×3" piece of heavy cardboard
6×3" piece of antique blue felt
Fabric or all-purpose glue
Pin back

stitches

Center and stitch the portion of the Holiday Evening Bag chart indicated by the dotted line onto the linen. Use three plies of floss to work the stitches over one square of fabric unless otherwise specified. Press the stitched piece from the back.

continued

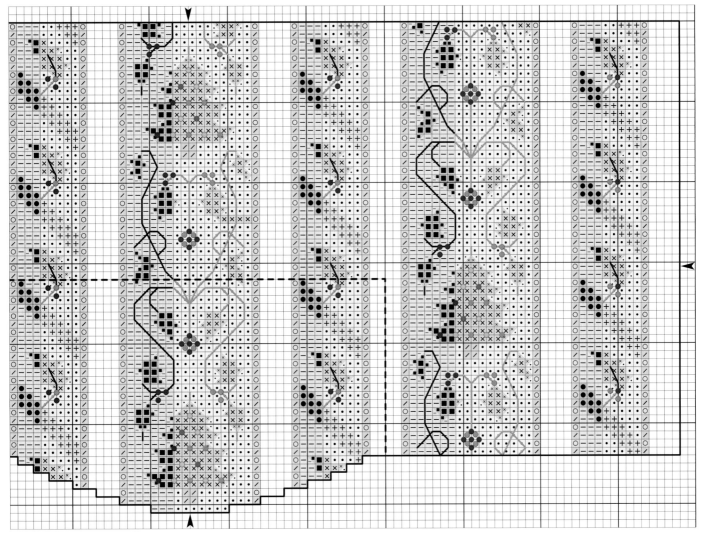

assembly

Use the erasable marker to transfer the dotted line to the stitched piece. To make a pattern, lay tracing paper over the stitched piece and trace the marker line; cut out. Cut out the stitched piece ½" beyond the dotted line. Use the pattern to cut one piece each from the fleece, cardboard, and felt.

Glue the fleece to the cardboard. Center the stitched piece on the fleece, turn the raw edges to the back, and glue. Glue the felt to the back side of the cardboard. Use all-purpose glue to attach the pin back.

Princess and Prince Ornaments

supplies

For each ornament
9" square of 36-count cream
    Edinburgh linen
Cotton embroidery floss
Kreinik #4 very fine braid
Erasable fabric marker
Tracing paper
4" square of self-stick mounting board
    with foam
4" square of cream felt
½ yard of ⅛"-diameter metallic gold
    twisted cord
Crafts glue

stitches

Center and stitch the Royal Needle Case chart on the linen. Use one ply of floss or one strand of braid to work the stitches over two threads of the fabric unless otherwise specified. Press the stitched piece from the back.

assembly

Use the erasable fabric marker to transfer the outline indicated by the dotted line on the chart; *do not* cut out. Place the tracing paper over the fabric and trace the drawn outline. Cut out the paper pattern and use it to cut shapes from the mounting board and felt.

Peel the protective paper from the mounting board. Center the foam side on the back of the stitched piece and press to stick. Trim the excess fabric ½" beyond the edge of the board. Fold the edge of the fabric to the back and glue in place.

Position and glue the cord around the edge of the ornament, overlapping the cord and forming a loop at the top center. Trim the excess cord and glue the ends to the ornament back. Glue the felt to the back of the ornament.

Royal Needle Case

supplies

2—9" squares of 35-count ivory linen
Cotton embroidery floss
Kreinik #4 very fine braid
Tracing paper
6×10" piece of gold lining fabric
4×8" piece of lightweight cardboard
9×12" piece of ivory felt
Matching sewing thread
Emery
1½ yards of ⅛"-wide ivory satin ribbon
Sharp sewing needle

stitches

Center and stitch each chart on one square of linen. Use one ply of floss or one strand of braid to work the stitches over two threads of the fabric unless otherwise specified. Use two plies of dark yellow-beige (DMC 3045) floss to backstitch an outline around the stitched area of each design as indicated by the dashed line on the charts. Press the stitched pieces from the back.

assembly

Trace the strawberry emery and the needle pad patterns, *opposite*, onto the tracing paper. To make the bell pattern, place tracing paper over one of the stitched pieces and trace the backstitch outline. Cut out the paper patterns.

Trim the stitched pieces ½" beyond the backstitch outline. Use a trimmed stitched piece as a pattern to cut two matching shapes from the lining fabric. Use the bell pattern to cut two shapes each from the cardboard and felt; trim the cardboard shapes slightly smaller

than the outlined shape. Cut one strawberry piece from the linen scraps. Cut one needle pad from felt.

To make a bell half, sew a row of gathering stitches about ¼" beyond the outline of the stitched piece. Glue a felt shape onto one cardboard shape. Center the felt side of the cardboard shape on the back of a stitched design. Pull the threads so the fabric edges are gathered evenly onto the back of the cardboard shape; knot the threads. Repeat for the second bell half.

Press under ½" along the top and bottom edges of the lining pieces. With wrong sides together, place one lining piece on each bell half. To finish the opening edges, use two plies of dark yellow-beige (DMC 3045) floss to slip-stitch the lining to the bell half for ½" at the top center and 2½" at the bottom. Make tiny stitches, taking one stitch in each backstitch. Trim the excess seam allowances on the side edges of the lining pieces.

For the strawberry, press under ⅜", first at the point, and then along one straight edge as indicated on the pattern. Fold the berry in half with the pressed edge overlapping the opposite edge; slip-stitch in place. Sew a row of gathering stitches ¼" from the curved edge of berry. Fill the strawberry with emery. Tighten the gathering threads, adding emery to round out the top of the strawberry. Pull the threads tightly until there is almost no opening at the top; knot securely. Use six plies of dark yellow-beige floss to make a ribbed spiderweb stitch on the top of the berry, referring to the diagram, *opposite*.

Cut two 18" lengths of ribbon. Fold the felt needle pad in half. Referring to the pattern, position the ribbons on one half of the needle pad, leaving 4" tails at the bottom edge. Sew the ribbons to the top layer of felt. To attach the straw berry, thread the 4" ribbon tails through the center of the spider stitch and knot the ribbons.

Sew the bell halves together with two plies of dark yellow-beige floss and a sharp sewing needle, making tiny stitches that each catch the ribbon edge and one backstitch. Sew a 5" length of ribbon to the side edge of a bell half, turning under ½" at the beginning and end of the ribbon. With the wrong side of the bell halves together, sew the opposite edge of the ribbon to the second bell half in the same manner. Place the felt needle pad between the bell halves. Sew the second ribbon length to the remaining side edges of the bell halves. This will create a small opening at the top center and a larger opening along the bottom.

To create channels for the ribbons, use dark yellow-beige floss to divide the top center opening in half with a ribbon in each half. With the felt needle pad inside the bell, tie a knot in the ribbons 2" above the bell. Tie a second knot 2" from the first knot. Pull the berry to slide the felt needle pad out of the bell and pull the top ribbons to slide the needle pad into the bell.

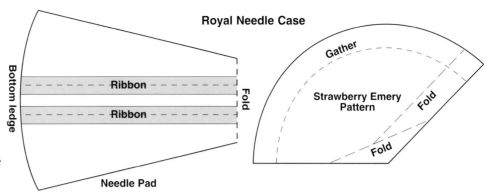

Royal Needle Case

Ribbon
Ribbon

Bottom ledge
Fold
Needle Pad

Gather
Strawberry Emery Pattern
Fold
Fold

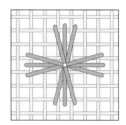

Diamond Eye Variation

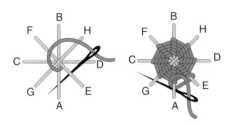

Ribbed Spiderweb

Royal Needle Case–Blue

Anchor		DMC	
897	♥	221	Deep shell pink
893	•	224	Light shell pink
1035	♦	930	Dark antique blue
1034	✕	931	Medium antique blue
887	◉	3045	Dark yellow-beige
886	□	3046	Medium yellow-beige
236	■	3799	Charcoal
	⁄	002	Kreinik Gold very fine #4 braid

STRAIGHT STITCH

887	⁄	3045	Dark yellow-beige – strawberry seeds (1X)
236	⁄	3799	Charcoal – facial features (1X)

DIAMOND EYELET VARIATION

886	✳	3046	Medium yellow-beige – queen's gown (1X)

Stitch count: 54 high x 51 wide

Finished design sizes:
36-count fabric – 3 x 2⅞ inches
32-count fabric – 3⅜ x 3⅛ inches
28-count fabric – 3⅞ x 3⅝ inches

Royal Needle Case–Green

Anchor		DMC	
893	•	224	Light shell pink
102	♥	550	Violet
887	◉	3045	Dark yellow-beige
886	□	3046	Medium yellow-beige
681	♦	3051	Dark gray-green
858	✕	3053	Light gray-green
236	■	3799	Charcoal
	⁄	002	Kreinik Gold very fine #4 braid

STRAIGHT STITCH

887	⁄	3045	Dark yellow-beige – strawberry seeds (1X)
236	⁄	3799	Charcoal – facial features (1X)

DIAMOND EYELET VARIATION

886	✳	3046	Medium yellow-beige – queen's gown (1X)

Royal Needle Case–Back

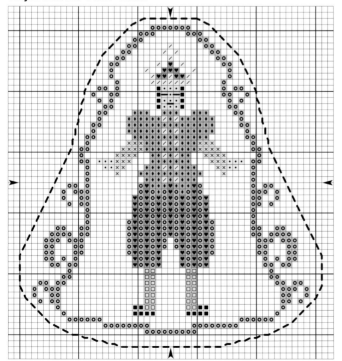

Royal Needle Case–Front

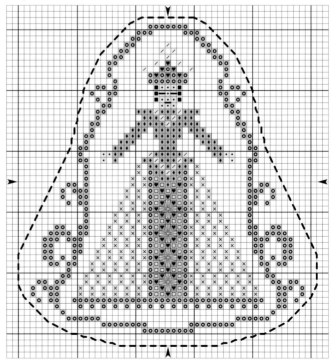

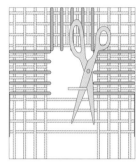

Satin Stitch

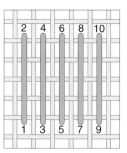

Removing Threads

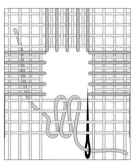

Woven Bars

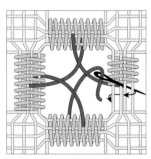

Dove's Eye

Vienna Rose Pillow

supplies

16" square of seafoam green 22-count
  Vienna fabric
Cotton embroidery floss
#5 and #8 ecru pearl cotton
⅜ yard of 45"-wide pink cotton fabric
1⅜ yards of ⅜"-diameter cream sew-in
  twisted cording
Matching sewing thread
Polyester fiberfill

stitches

Center and stitch the chart on the Vienna
fabric. Use four plies of floss to work the
cross-stitches over two threads of the
fabric. Work the backstitches with two
plies of floss. Referring to the diagrams,
work the satin-stitch kloster blocks using
one strand of #5 pearl cotton over the
number of threads indicated on the
chart. Cut and remove the threads for the
woven areas of the design as indicated
on the chart. Use one strand of #8 pearl
cotton to work the woven bars and
dove's eyes over the exposed threads.
Press the stitched piece from the back.

assembly

Centering the design, trim the stitched
piece to a 12¼" square. From the pink

fabric, cut two 12¼" squares for the
underlining and back. All measurements
include a ½" seam allowance.

For the pillow front, place the stitched
piece, wrong side down, on the right
side of the pink underlining square;
baste the raw edges together along the
seam line. Use a zipper foot to sew the
cream cording to the front of the
stitched piece.

Sew the pillow front and back together
with right sides facing, slightly rounding
the corners and leaving an opening for
turning. Trim the seams, clip the corners,
and turn right side out. Press. Stuff the
pillow firmly with polyester fiberfill and
slip-stitch the opening closed.

Rose Eyeglass Case

supplies

3½×7" Stitch & Zip eyeglass case with
  14-count Aida cloth insert
Cotton embroidery floss

stitches

Center and stitch the rose motif on the
Aida cloth insert. Use three plies of floss
to work the cross-stitches over one
square of fabric.

Vienna Rose Pillow

Anchor		DMC (4X)
217	▲	367 Pistachio
039	◉	961 Dark rose-pink
075	☒	962 Medium rose-pink
073	•	963 Pale rose-pink
243	✛	988 Forest green
059	♥	3350 Dusty rose
025	＝	3716 Light rose-pink

SATIN STITCH

926 ▥ Ecru #5 pearl cotton –
border around rose (1X)

Anchor		DMC
BACKSTITCH		
217	／	367 Pistachio – stem (2X)
WOVEN BARS		
926	▥	Ecru #8 pearl cotton (1X)
DOVE'S EYE		
926	✂	Ecru #8 pearl cotton (1X)

Stitch count: *110 high x 110 wide*

Finished design sizes:
22-count fabric – 10 x 10 inches
28-count fabric – 7⅞ x 7⅞ inches
32-count fabric – 6⅞ x 6⅞ inches

Algerian Eyelet

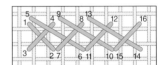

Doubleback Stitch

Work of Mine
Book Cover

supplies

10" square of 28-count platinum
   Cashel linen
Gentle Art Sampler Threads
   overdyed floss
¼ yard of burgundy cotton fabric
¼ yard of lightweight fleece
Matching sewing thread
Purchased 5¾×6½×1¼" address or
   photo book
1¼ yards of ⅜"-wide ribbon

stitches

Center and stitch the chart on the linen.
Use two plies of floss to work the
stitches over two threads of the fabric
unless otherwise specified. When working with overdyed floss, complete each
individual stitch before proceeding to
the next one. Refer to the diagrams to
work the remaining stitches. Press the
stitched piece from the back.

assembly

Centering the design, trim the stitched
piece to a 5½" square.

From the burgundy fabric, cut a
7½×11" lining piece, a 7½×8½" left
side/back piece, two 2×5½" top and
bottom sashing strips, a 1¾×7½" right
sashing strip, and two 3¾×7½" inside
pockets. All measurements include a
½" seam allowance.

With right sides together, sew the
2×5½" sashing strips to the top and
bottom edges of the stitched piece.
Press seam allowances toward the
sashing. Sew the 1¾×7½" sashing strip to
the right edge of the stitched piece in
the same manner. Then, sew the left
side/back piece to the left edge of the
stitched piece.

Using the pieced fabric cover as a
pattern, cut one from fleece. Center and
baste the fleece to the wrong side of
the cover.

Cut the ⅜"-wide ribbon in half. On
the right side of the cover, sew a ribbon
piece centered on each short edge. Press

under ¼" twice on one long edge of
each inside pocket; topstitch close to the
first fold. Pin an inside pocket to one
short edge of the cover with right sides
together; sew. Repeat for the opposite
edge of the cover.

With right sides together, center the
lining on the cover; sew along the top
and bottom edges only. Trim the seams
and clip the corners; turn right side out
and press. Slip the ends of the book into
the pockets. Tie the ribbon into a bow.

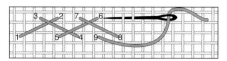

Herringbone Stitch

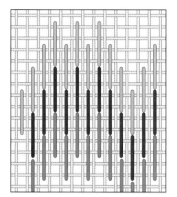

Florentine Stitch

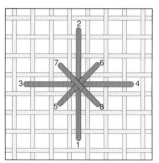

Star Stitch

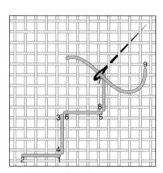

Fagot Stitch step 1

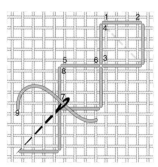

Fagot Stitch step 2

Work of Mine

Anchor		DMC		Gentle Art Sampler Threads
858	▲	3053	Gray-green	0110 Dried thyme
897	⊙	902	Garnet	0360 Cranberry
372	✕	422	Hazel	0540 Brandy
1012	✚	948	Peach	1160 Adobe

FAGOT STITCH

858		3053	Gray-green—leaves	0110 Dried thyme

ALGERIAN EYELET

897	✳	902	Garnet—corners	0360 Cranberry

DOUBLEBACK STITCH

858	✕✕✕	3053	Gray-green—border	0110 Dried thyme

HERRINGBONE STITCH

1012	✕✕	948	Peach	1160 Adobe

STAR STITCH

897	✳	902	Garnet	0360 Cranberry

FLORENTINE STITCH

858	▯▯	3053	Gray-green	0110 Dried thyme
897	▯▯	902	Garnet	0360 Cranberry
1012	▯▯	948	Peach	1160 Adobe

Stitch count: 61 high x 61 wide
Finished design sizes:
28-count fabric – 4⅜ x 4⅜ inches
32-count fabric – 3⅞ x 3⅞ inches
36-count fabric – 3⅜ x 3⅜ inches

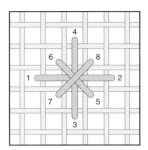

Star Stitch

Scarf, Hat, and Mitten Patches

supplies
For each patch
Purchased 14-count Aida cloth patch
Cotton embroidery floss
Matching sewing thread

stitches
Center and stitch the chart on the patch.
Use three plies of floss to work the
stitches over one square unless otherwise
specified. Press the finished stitchery
from the back. Sew the patch onto the
scarf, hat, or mitten with matching
sewing thread.

Reindeer Patch

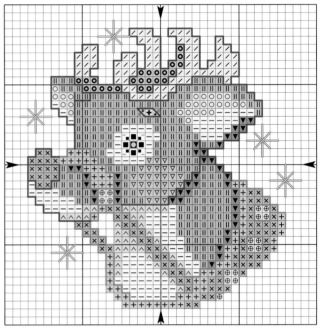

Santa Patch

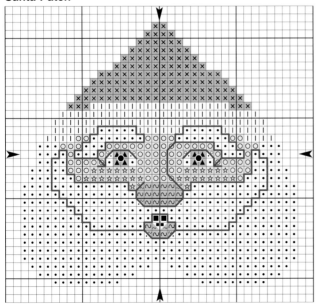

Elf Patch

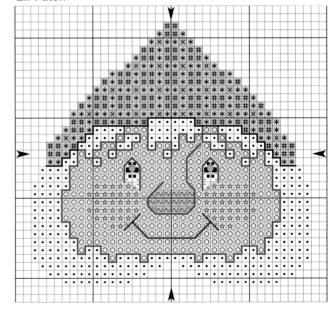

Santa, Reindeer, and Elf Patches

Anchor		DMC	
002	⋅	000	White
403	■	310	Black
9046	⊠	321	Christmas red
009	▽	352	Coral
235	✚	414	Dark steel
297	✳	444	Lemon
231	⌃	453	Shell gray
227	#	701	Christmas green
590	−	712	Cream
137	▲	798	Delft blue
257	✚	905	Parrot green
882	○	945	Ivory
026	☆	957	Geranium
297	⊕	973	Canary
1001	II	976	Medium golden brown
1098	∿	3801	Watermelon
3058	◹	3821	True straw
1048	▼	3826	Dark golden brown
305	◉	3852	Deep straw

BLENDED-NEEDLE
002	⊡	000	White (2X) and
		032	Kreinik pearl blending filament (2X)

BACKSTITCH
403	╱	310	Black – elf hat (1X)
404	╱	321	Christmas red – elf mouth (2X)
235	╱	414	Dark steel – Santa and elf beard and facial details, reindeer body (1X); elf and Santa eyes (2X)
	╱	002	Kreinik gold #4 very-fine braid – reindeer reins and collar (1X)

FRENCH KNOT
002	●	000	White – elf eye highlight (1X wrapped once)
403	●	310	Black – Santa's pupils (2X wrapped three times)
590	●	712	Cream – reindeer eye highlight (1X wrapped once)

STAR STITCH
	✳	002	Kreinik gold #4 very-fine braid – stars on reindeer patch

Santa Patch stitch count: *33 high x 36 wide*
Santa Patch finished design sizes:
14-count fabric – 2 1/3 x 2 1/2 inches
16-count fabric – 2 x 2 1/4 inches
18-count fabric – 1 7/8 x 2 inches

Elf Patch stitch count: *33 high x 36 wide*
Elf Patch finished design sizes:
14-count fabric – 2 1/3 x 2 1/2 inches
16-count fabric – 2 x 2 1/4 inches
18-count fabric – 1 7/8 x 2 inches

Reindeer Patch stitch count: *36 high x 36 wide*
Reindeer Patch finished design sizes:
14-count fabric – 2 1/2 x 2 1/2 inches
16-count fabric – 2 1/4 x 2 1/4 inches
18-count fabric – 2 x 2 inches

Season's Greetings Toy Sampler

The chart and key are on pages 80–81.

supplies
12×16" piece of 14-count white Aida cloth
Cotton embroidery floss
Desired frame

stitches
Center and stitch the chart on the fabric using three plies of floss to work the stitches over one square unless otherwise specified. Press the finished stitchery from the back. Frame as desired.

Row of Hearts Bib

The chart and key are on pages 80–81.

supplies
Purchased denim bib with a 2 1/4"-wide 14-count Aida-cloth insert
Cotton embroidery floss

stitches
Center and stitch the heart row from the Season's Greetings Toy Sampler chart on the Aida-cloth bib insert, eliminating the partial hearts at the beginning and end of the row. Use three plies of floss to work the stitches over one square. Press the finished bib from the back.

Train Overalls

supplies

14-count 2¼"-wide blue-and-white floral Aida cloth banding 1" longer than the width of the overall bib
Cotton embroidery floss
Purchased child's overalls

stitches

Center and stitch the train from the Season's Greetings Toy Sampler chart on the banding, eliminating the French knots between cars. Use three plies of floss to work the stitches over one square unless otherwise specified. Use black (DMC 310) for the French knot on the engine's large wheel. Press the stitched piece from the back. Sew banding across the top of the overalls.

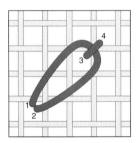

Lazy Daisy

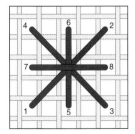

Smyrna Cross

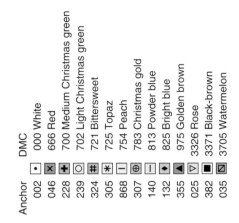

Anchor	DMC	
002	000	White
046	666	Red
228	700	Medium Christmas green
239	702	Light Christmas green
324	721	Bittersweet
305	725	Topaz
868	754	Peach
307	783	Christmas gold
140	813	Powder blue
132	825	Bright blue
355	975	Golden brown
025	3326	Rose
382	3371	Black-brown
035	3705	Watermelon

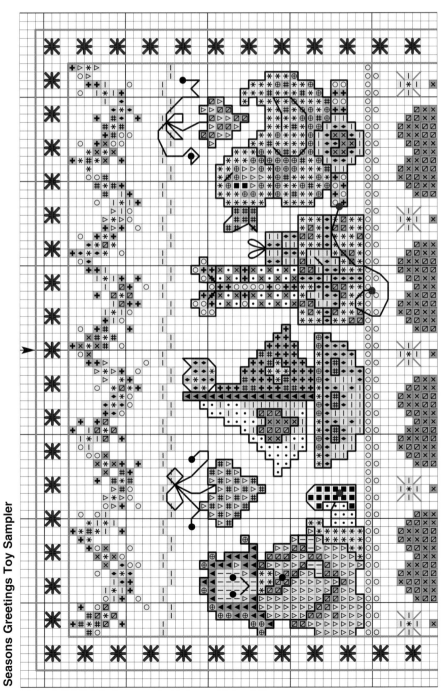

Seasons Greetings Toy Sampler

BACKSTITCH

046	⁄	666 Red – small boxes under lettering, doll socks (1X)
228	⁄	700 Medium Christmas green – blue flower leaves, yellow flower leaves, trees at bottom, border (1X)
307	⁄	783 Christmas gold – design under lettering (1X)
140	⁄	813 Powder blue – snowflakes near lettering (1X)
132	⁄	825 Bright blue – snowflakes over large trees (1X), lettering (2X)
382	⁄	3371 Black-brown – all other stitches (1X)

FRENCH KNOT

046	●	666 Red – button on doll shoe, ends of pull toy string, center of large train wheel (2X wrapped once)
132	●	825 Bright blue – snowflakes over large trees, apostrophe and "i" in lettering (1X wrapped once)
382	●	3371 Black-brown – doll eyes, button on doll dress, ends of heart strings, chains between train cars (2X wrapped once)

LAZY DAISY

| 382 | 𝒪 | 3371 Black-brown – bow on package (1X) |

SMYRNA CROSS-STITCH

| 046 | ✳ | 666 Red – outer border |
| 324 | ✳ | 721 Bittersweet – bottom of small tree row |

Sampler stitch count: 132 high x 76 wide
Sampler finished design sizes:
14-count fabric – 9³⁄₈ x 5³⁄₈ inches
16-count fabric – 8¼ x 4¾ inches
18-count fabric – 7¹⁄₃ x 4¼ inches

Bib stitch count: 10 high x 59 wide
Bib finished design sizes:
14-count fabric – ³⁄₄ x 4¼ inches

Banding stitch count: 13 high x 43 wide
Banding finished design sizes:
14-count fabric – 1 x 3 inches
16-count fabric – ⁷⁄₈ x 2²⁄₃ inches
18-count fabric – ³⁄₄ x 2³⁄₈ inches

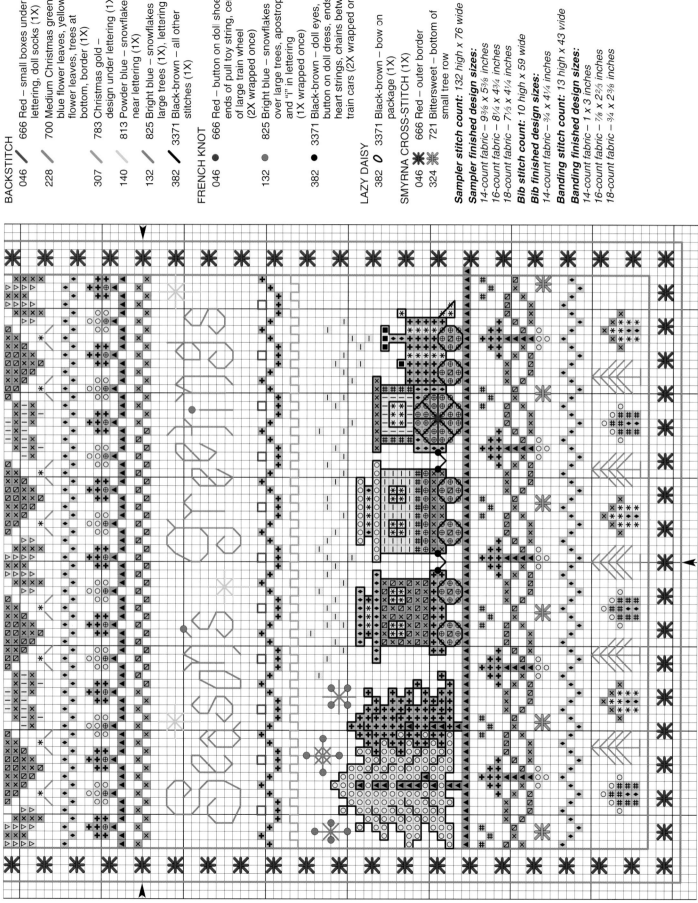

Traditions

Renewed

Holiday traditions lovingly bind family, friends, and neighbors together. Simple or extravagant, shared for generations, or newly celebrated, they keep the spirit of Christmas alive. This year, freshen up an old family favorite or create a new tradition with one of these enchanting ideas.

*O*ne of childhood's greatest anticipations *is the countdown to Christmas and marking off the days on a calendar. This treat-laden design dispenses peppermints tied to each December day from the 1st through the 24th. Stitched in pearl cotton on 16-count linen, it's finished quilt-style with sashing and a rod pocket on the back for hanging. For fun, trim the snowman's cap with angora-thread stitches. Add black buttons for "coal" eyes and a mouth.*

Project instructions begin on page 92.
Design: Deborah Brewer of Frances & Me. Photograph: Scott Little

*R*efresh an old Pennsylvania Dutch *needlework tradition and decorate your walls in this cheery red and white adaptation of a show towel. With roots traced as far back as 15th-century Germany, the original towels were long, thin banners meant for showcasing an embroiderer's repertoire—not for drying hands!*

Project instructions begin on page 94.
Design: Johannah Adams of Window Garden Designs. Photograph: Scott Little

*S*hare a cup of tea with family and good friends, and make it a holiday tradition with enticing foods and fabulous decorations like these. The gingerbread cozy keeps your beverage warm and sets the theme for your table. Decorated in beaded candies and holiday motifs, it looks good enough to eat. For other table accoutrements, lift small portions of the design. We added the wreath to a napkin, then ringed it in poinsettias, piping, and red rickrack.

　　　You've trimmed the table. Now, trim yourself! Turn to page 99 for a sparkling poinsettia pin made of multifaceted beads.

Project instructions begin on page 98.
Design: Barbara Sestok. Photographs: Marcia Cameron and Steve Struse

*O*ne of the most beloved and often-performed *ballets* during the holidays, The Nutcracker *tells the story of a girl named Clara and the nutcracker she's given for a Christmas present. Share the tale and one of these soft nutcracker soldiers with your own little "Clara." Done on easy 11-count Aida, both dolls are worked from one chart with two color keys.*

Project begins on page 102.
Design: Juliet Anne Jones of Cat's Cradle Needlework. Photographs: Scott Little

The tradition of stockings is as old as Santa Claus himself, so the story goes. For three nights, St. Nicholas left small bags of gold at the home of a needy family. One evening, he dropped the gold down the chimney where it landed in a stocking hung by the fire to dry! Much finer than that first gold-filled stocking, this one is a needlework masterpiece. Stitched on 32-count linen, it's covered in an elaborate village of 18th-century-style houses.

Project instructions begin opposite.
Design: Mike Vickery of Vickery Designs. Photograph: Steve Struse

Christmas Village Stocking

The chart and key are on pages 90–91.

supplies

13×16" piece of 28-count spun
 silver linen
Cotton embroidery floss
Graph paper; pencil
9×12" piece of fusible fleece
Erasable fabric marker
³⁄₈ yard of 45"-wide coordinating cotton
 fabric
⁷⁄₈ yard of ³⁄₁₆"-diameter cording
Matching sewing thread

stitches

Use the alphabet, *right,* to chart the
desired name on graph paper, separating
each letter with one square.

Center and stitch the chart on the
linen. Use two plies of floss to work the
stitches over two threads of the fabric
unless otherwise specified. Press the
stitched piece from the back.

assembly

Center and fuse the fleece to the back
of the stitched piece following the
manufacturer's instructions. Use the
erasable fabric marker to draw the
stocking outline around the stitched area
of the design as indicated by the dotted
line on the chart. Cut out the stocking
shape ¹⁄₂" beyond the marked outline.

Use the trimmed stitched piece as a
pattern to cut a matching back and two
lining pieces from the coordinating
fabric. From the same fabric, cut a 1¹⁄₂×6"
hanging strip and enough 1⁵⁄₈"-wide bias
strips to make 30" of piping.

Sew the short ends of the piping
strips together to make one long strip.
Center the cording lengthwise on the
wrong side of the piping strip. Fold the
fabric around the cording with the long
edges together. Use a zipper foot to sew
through both layers close to the cording.
Baste the piping around the sides and
foot of the stocking front with the raw
edges even.

With right sides together and using
the zipper foot, sew the stocking front to
the back along the basting lines, leaving
the top edge open. Trim the seams, clip
the curves, and turn right side out. Press.

Press under ¹⁄₄" on the long edges of
the 1¹⁄₂×6" hanging strip, fold it in half
lengthwise, and topstitch. Fold the strip
in half to form a loop. Sew the loop to
the top right corner of the stocking with
the raw edges even.

continued

Christmas Village Alphabet

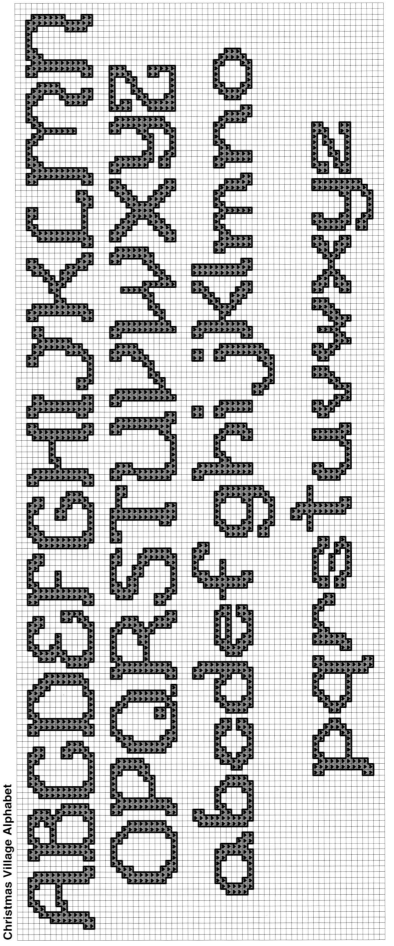

With right sides facing, sew the lining pieces together with a ½" seam allowance, leaving the top edge open and an opening on one side for turning. Trim the seams and clip the curves, but *do not* turn. Slip the stocking inside the lining with right sides together. Sew the stocking and lining together at the top edge. Trim the seam and turn right side out. Slip-stitch the opening closed. Tuck the lining into the stocking and press carefully.

Christmas Village Stocking

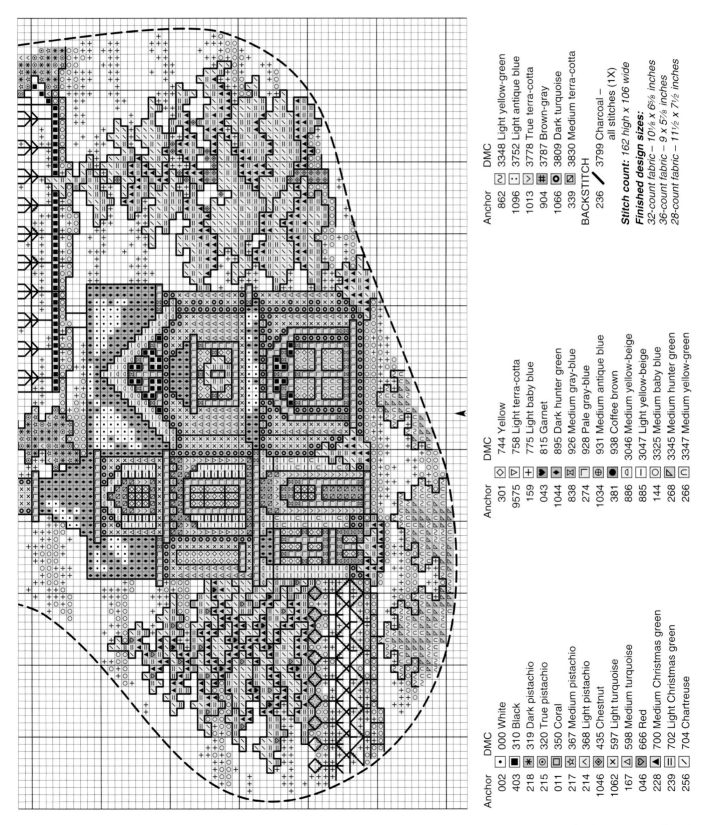

Anchor		DMC
301	◇	744 Yellow
9575	▽	758 Light terra-cotta
159	+	775 Light baby blue
043	◐	815 Garnet
1044	◆	895 Dark hunter green
838	⊠	926 Medium gray-blue
274	⌐	928 Pale gray-blue
1034	⊕	931 Medium antique blue
381	●	938 Coffee brown
886	◁	3046 Medium yellow-beige
885	—	3047 Light yellow-beige
144	○	3325 Medium baby blue
268	◤	3345 Medium hunter green
266	∩	3347 Medium yellow-green

Anchor		DMC
002	•	000 White
403	■	310 Black
218	✱	319 Dark pistachio
215	⊙	320 True pistachio
011	☐	350 Coral
217	☆	367 Medium pistachio
214	<	368 Light pistachio
1046	◈	435 Chestnut
1062	✕	597 Light turquoise
167	◁	598 Medium turquoise
046	◇	666 Red
228	◀	700 Medium Christmas green
239	⫴	702 Light Christmas green
256	/	704 Chartreuse

Anchor		DMC
862	⊵	3348 Light yellow-green
1096	⫶	3752 Light antique blue
1013	▷	3778 True terra-cotta
904	#	3787 Brown-gray
1066	◉	3809 Dark turquoise
339	⊘	3830 Medium terra-cotta

BACKSTITCH

236	╱	3799 Charcoal – all stitches (1X)

Stitch count: 162 high x 106 wide

Finished design sizes:
32-count fabric – 10⅛ x 6⅝ inches
36-count fabric – 9 x 5⅞ inches
28-count fabric – 11½ x 7½ inches

Counting the Days

DMC #5 Pearl Cotton

⊡	000 White
■	310 Black
✕	321 Christmas red
╱	413 Pewter
∧	740 Tangerine
♡	760 Salmon
◆	823 Navy
◉	890 Pistachio
◯	931 Antique blue

HALF CROSS-STITCH (1X)
(stitch in direction of symbol)

╱	SB1 White Rainbow Gallery – hat trim

BACKSTITCH (1X)

╱	000 White – snow
╱	310 Black – all other stitches

BLENDED-NEEDLE STRAIGHT STITCH

╱	823 Navy (1X) and 931 Antique blue (1X) – scarf

SURFACE ATTACHMENTS

✕	86355U Mill Hill small mocha red star button
✕	86357U Mill Hill large mocha red star button
●	⅛"-diameter black shank button – eyes and mouth
○	⅜"-diameter black faceted shank button – jacket

Stitch count: 142 high x 124 wide

Finished design sizes:
8-count fabric – 17¾ x 15½ inches
14-count fabric – 10⅛ x 8⅞ inches
16-count fabric – 8¾ x 7¾ inches

Counting the Days

supplies
22×27" piece of 16-count natural Betsy Ross linen
#5 pearl cotton
Rainbow Gallery Santa's Beard and Suit thread
1 large red ceramic star button
1 small red ceramic star button
3—⅜"-diameter black buttons
7—³⁄₁₆"-diameter black buttons
18×22" piece (fat quarter) of blue plaid fabric
18×22" piece (fat quarter) of green print fabric
⅜ yard of red fabric
⅝ yard of backing fabric
27×32" of quilt batting
6 yards of ⅛"-wide green ribbon
Red-and-white-striped candies

stitches
Center and stitch the design from the chart on the fabric. Use one strand of pearl cotton to work the cross-stitches over two threads of the fabric unless otherwise specified. Work the remaining stitches as specified in the key. Sew on buttons as indicated on the chart.

assembly
All seams are ¼" wide unless otherwise specified. Centering the design, trim the stitched piece to measure 17½×22". From both the blue plaid and the green print fabrics, cut six 2½×22" border strips. From the red fabric, cut four 2¼" corner squares and three 2½×42" binding strips. From the backing fabric cut a 27×32" back and a 20×4½" hanging sleeve.

Sew the long edges of the blue plaid and green print strips together alternating colors (see Bias Strip Diagram). Press seams open. Starting at one corner of the joined strips, use a ruler and a rotary cutter to cut across the strip at a 45-degree angle. Rotary-cut parallel to the first cut to make four 2¼"-wide striped-border strips. (Or use an

air-soluble marker to draw diagonal lines. Cut along the lines with scissors.)

Trim two of the striped-border strips to the same length as the sides of the stitched piece (22"). Sew a striped-border piece to each side of the stitched piece. Press the seam allowances toward the border.

Trim the remaining striped-border strips to the length of the top and bottom of the stitched piece (17½").

continued

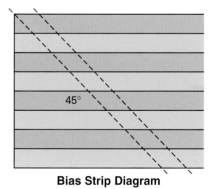

45°

Bias Strip Diagram

Counting the Days

Sew a red corner square to both ends of each strip. Press the seam allowances toward the corners. Sew one striped-border piece to the top and one to the bottom of the stitched center. Press the seam allowances toward the border.

Place the quilt back, right side down, on a smooth surface. Center and smooth the batting on the back. Center the pieced quilt top on the batting; baste through all layers.

Hand- or machine-quilt a grid forming a rectangle around each number. Also quilt in the ditch (on the seam lines) along the seams of the border. Trim the back and batting even with the front. Fold the short ends of the hanging strip under ¼" twice to form a narrow hem; topstitch close to the first fold. Fold the strip in half lengthwise, wrong sides together. Center the raw edges of the folded strip along the top edge of the quilted center; baste along the seam line. Join the binding strips with diagonal seams to make one long binding strip. Press the seam allowances open. Fold the binding strip in half lengthwise, wrong sides together, and press. Aligning the raw edges of the binding strip and the quilt top, pin and stitch the binding to the right side of the top, mitering the corners. Turn the folded edge of the binding over the raw edges to the back. Hand-stitch the binding's folded edge to the backing fabric. Cut ribbon into 24—8" lengths. Tack onto stitched piece, centering one length under each number. Tie a candy onto the piece with each ribbon.

Show Towel-Style Stocking

The chart and key are on pages 96–97.

Supplies

15×18" piece of 28-count antique white
   Cashel linen
Cotton embroidery floss
Graph paper; pencil
11×14" piece of fusible fleece
Erasable fabric marker
½ yard of 45"-wide white cotton fabric
⅛ yard of 45"-wide red cotton fabric
1 yard of ⅛"-diameter cording
Matching sewing threads

stitches

Use the alphabet to chart the desired name on graph paper, separating each letter with three squares.

Center and stitch the chart on the linen. Use three plies of floss to work the stitches over two threads of the fabric unless otherwise specified. Press the stitched piece from the back.

assembly

Center and fuse the fleece to the back of the stitched piece following the manufacturer's instructions. Use the erasable fabric marker to draw the stocking outline around the stitched area of the design as indicated by the dotted line on the chart. Cut out the stocking shape ½" beyond the marked outline.

Use the trimmed stitched piece as a pattern to cut a matching back and two lining pieces from the white fabric. From the red fabric, cut a 1½×6" hanging strip and a 1⅜×36" piping strip.

Center the cording lengthwise on the wrong side of the piping strip. Fold the fabric around the cording with the long edges together. Use a zipper foot to sew through both layers close to the cording. Baste the piping around the sides and foot of the stocking front with the raw edges even.

With right sides together and using the zipper foot, sew the stocking front to the back along the basting lines, leaving the top edge open. Trim the seams, clip the curves, and turn right side out. Press.

Press under ¼" on the long edges of the 1½×6" hanging strip, fold it in half

lengthwise and topstitch. Fold the strip in half to form a loop. Sew the loop to the top right corner of the stocking with the raw edges even.

With right sides facing, sew the lining pieces together with a ½" seam allowance, leaving the top edge open and an opening on one side for turning. Trim the seams and clip the curves, but *do not* turn. Slip the stocking inside the lining with right sides together. Sew the stocking and lining together at the top edge. Trim the seam and turn right side out. Slip-stitch the opening closed. Tuck the lining into the stocking and press.

Show Towel-Style Alphabet

Anchor   DMC

1006 ⊠   304 Christmas red

Stitch count: *172 high x 113 wide*

Finished design sizes:

28-count fabric – 12¼ x 8 inches

32-count fabric – 10¾ x 7 inches

36-count fabric – 9½ x 6¼ inches

Show Towel-Style Stocking

Anchor	DMC	
1006	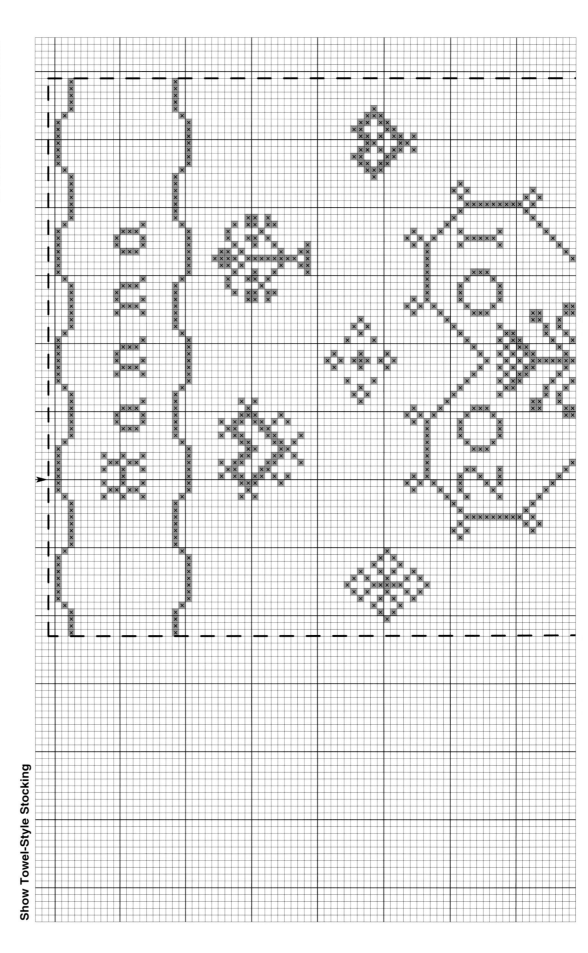 304	Christmas red

Stitch count: 172 high x 113 wide

Finished design sizes:
28-count fabric – 12¼ x 8 inches
32-count fabric – 10¾ x 7 inches
36-count fabric – 9½ x 6¼ inches

Show Towel-Style Stocking

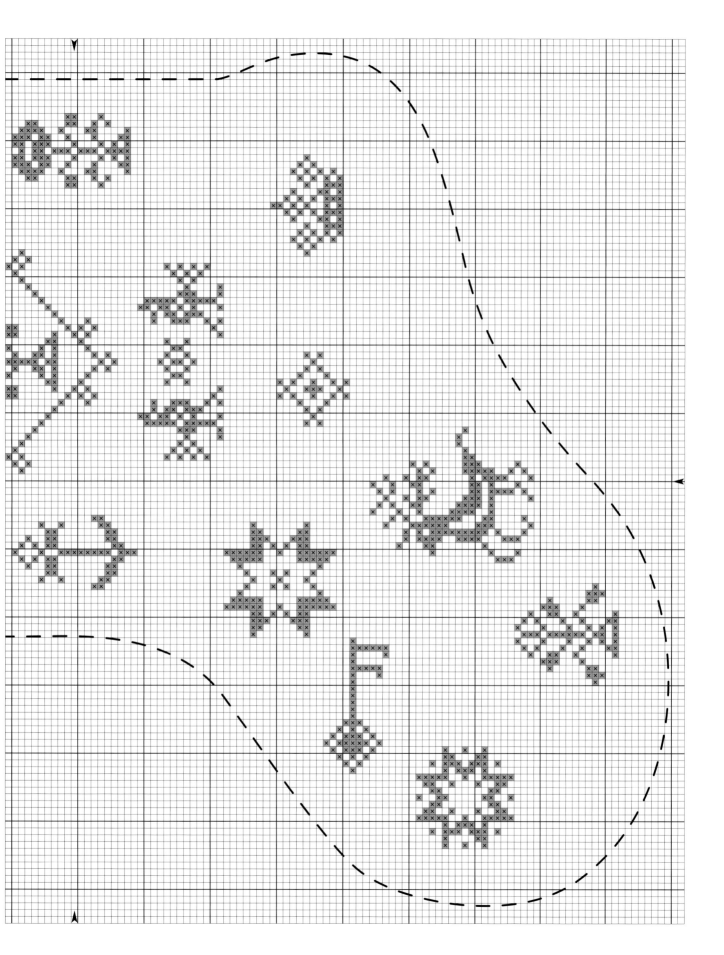

Gingerbread House Tea Cozy

The chart and key are on pages 100–101.

supplies

16×18" piece of 28-count coffee
 bean linen
Cotton embroidery floss
Mill Hill seed beads
14×28" piece of fleece
Erasable fabric marker
½ yard of 45"-wide red cotton fabric
30" length of red medium rickrack
4" length of red narrow rickrack
Matching sewing thread

stitches

Center and stitch the chart on the linen. Use three plies of floss to work the stitches over two threads of the fabric unless otherwise specified. Attach the seed beads using two plies of matching floss. Press the stitched piece from the back.

assembly

Use the erasable fabric marker to draw the tea cozy outline, marking ¼" beyond the scallops on the roof and along the outside lines of the chart on the sides and bottom. Cut out the tea cozy shape ½" beyond the marked outline.

Use the trimmed stitched piece as a pattern to cut two interlining pieces from the fleece and one back and two lining pieces from the red fabric.

Baste one piece of fleece to the wrong side of the stitched piece and the other to the red back. Baste the medium rickrack around the sides and top edges of the cozy front, centering the rickrack on the basting lines. Fold the 4" length of narrow rickrack in half to form a loop. Sew the loop to the top center front of the cozy back with the raw edges even.

With right sides together, sew the cozy front to the back along the basting lines, leaving the bottom edge open. Trim the seams and turn right side out.

Press. Sew the lining pieces together in the same manner, leaving the bottom edge open and an opening on one side for turning. Trim the seams, but *do not* turn.

Slip the cozy inside the lining with right sides together. Sew the cozy and lining together at the bottom edge. Trim the seam and turn right side out. Slip-stitch the opening closed. Tuck the lining into the cozy and press carefully.

Poinsettia Napkin Ring
The chart and key are on pages 100–101.

supplies
For each napkin ring
6×11" piece of 22-count Williamsburg green Janina fabric
Cotton embroidery floss
Mill Hill seed beads
25×9" piece of fleece
18" length of purchased ⅛"-diameter white sew-in piping
18" length of red medium rickrack
2½×9" piece of red cotton fabric
Matching sewing thread

stitches
Measure 2" in from one short edge of the fabric; begin stitching one poinsettia from the Gingerbread House Tea Cozy chart there, centering it horizontally on the fabric. Use three plies of floss to work the stitches over two threads of the fabric. Work the backstitches with one ply of floss. Continue stitching across the fabric, completing three pairs of leaves and four poinsettias. Attach the seed beads using two plies of matching floss. Press the stitched piece from the back.

assembly
Centering the design, trim the fabric to measure 2½×9". (Measurements include ¼" seam

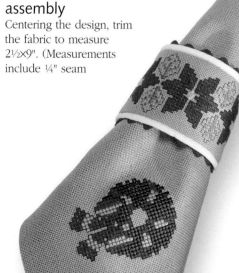

allowances unless otherwise specified.) Baste the fleece to the wrong side of the stitched piece. Cut the piping in half and use a zipper foot to sew one piece to each long edge of the stitched piece with raw edges even. Cut the rickrack in half and baste it atop the piping so the rickrack extends beyond the rounded edge of the piping. With right sides together, use a zipper foot to sew the red fabric to the stitched piece along the long edges. Trim the seams, turn right side out, and press. Zigzag-stitch the raw edges. With right sides of the stitched piece together, sew together the short ends using a ¾" seam allowance. Press the seam allowances open and tack in place.

Wreath Napkin
The chart and key are on pages 100–101.

supplies
For each napkin
18" square of 22-count Williamsburg green Janina fabric
Matching sewing thread
Cotton embroidery floss

stitches
Fold the edges of the fabric under ½" twice on all four sides; topstitch. Measure 2½" from the edges on one corner of the fabric; begin stitching the center of the door wreath from the Gingerbread House Tea Cozy chart there. Use three plies of floss to work the stitches over two threads of the fabric. Substitute a deep pistachio (DMC 890) cross-stitch for each bead. Work the backstitches with one ply of floss. Press the finished napkin from the back.

Poinsettia Brooch
The chart and key are on pages 100–101.

supplies
4" square of 14-count white or clear perforated plastic
Cotton embroidery floss
Mill Hill seed and Magnifica beads
Gold Ribbonfloss
¾"-long metal pin back

stitches
Center and stitch one poinsettia from the Gingerbread House Tea Cozy on the perforated plastic, using one ply of floss to work the backstitches first. Referring to the diagram and using two plies of floss, add a bead to each cross-stitch Trim the perforated plastic one square beyond the stitching. Use one strand of Ribbonfloss to work whipstitches around the outside edge of the plastic. Use matching floss to attach the pin back.

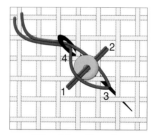

Attaching Beads

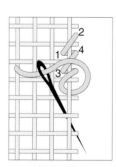

Whipstitch

Gingerbread House Tea Cozy

Anchor		DMC	
002	•	000	White
109	◎	209	Lavender
1006	♥	304	Christmas red
117	I	341	Periwinkle
288	−	445	Lemon
046	✕	666	Red
256	+	704	Chartreuse
302	/	743	Yellow
683	●	890	Deep pistachio
257	□	905	Parrot green
298	◉	972	Canary
328	⊞	3341	Melon
033	♡	3706	Watermelon

BACKSTITCH

109	/	209 Lavender – gumdrops (2X)
218	/	319 Dark pistachio – poinsettia leaves (2X)
288	/	445 Lemon – gumdrops (2X)
358	/	801 Coffee brown – wreath (2X), windows, door, and keyhole (1X)
897	/	902 Garnet – bow, red hearts, and poinsettias (2X)
257	/	905 Parrot green – vines (2X)
905	/	3021 Brown-gray – holly leaf veins (1X)
328	/	3341 Melon – gumdrops (2X)
033	/	3706 Watermelon – pink hearts around windows (1X)
306	/	3820 Straw – holly leaves, door knob (2X), and door knob plaquet (1X)

FRENCH KNOT (1X wrapped twice)

358	●	801 Coffee brown – keyhole

MILL HILL BEADS

	●	00148 Pale peach seed beads – poinsettia centers and wreath
	●	02013 Red red seed beads – holly berries
	●	40161 Crystal petite seed beads – gumdrops

Stitch count: 148 high x 165 wide

Finished design sizes:
28-count fabric – 10½ x 11¾ inches
32-count fabric – 9¼ x 10⅓ inches
36-count fabric – 8¼ x 9⅛ inches

Poinsettia Brooch

Mill Hill Beads

♥	03058 Mardi Gras red antique glass bead
●	10036 Victorian gold Magnifica bead
✕	10071 Opalescent cinnamon red Magnifica bead

Gingerbread House Tea Cozy

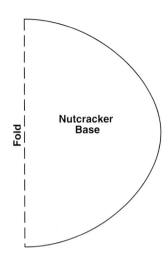

Nutcracker
Base

Fold

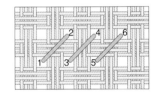

French Knot

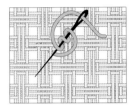

Half Cross-Stitch

Nutcracker Dolls

supplies

For one doll

5×10" piece of 11-count white Aida cloth
Cotton embroidery floss
Rainbow Gallery Whisper
Kreinik #8 fine braid
Erasable marker
6" square of tracing paper
¼ yard of blue or green print fabric
⅝ yard of ⅛"-diameter cording
Sewing thread to match fabrics
Polyester fiberfill
Plastic pellets
Small plastic bag; rubber band

stitches

Center and stitch the chart on the fabric. Use three plies of floss or one strand of braid to work the cross-stitches over one square. Use one strand of Whisper to work the half cross-stitches. Press the stitched piece from the back.

assembly

Referring to the photograph, *above*, use the erasable marker to draw an outline 1" beyond the stitching. Cut out ½" beyond the drawn line. Use the stitched piece as a pattern to cut a back from the print fabric. Fold the tracing paper in half. Trace the base pattern, *above*. Unfold the base pattern and draw around it on the print fabric. Cut out ½" beyond the drawn line. From the remaining print fabric cut enough 1⅜"-wide strips to equal 20".

Sew the short ends of the piping strips together to make one long piece. Center the cording lengthwise on the wrong side of the piping strip. Fold the fabric around the cording with the long edges together. Use a zipper foot to sew through both layers close to the cording. Baste the piping around the top and sides of the stitched piece with the raw edges even.

With right sides together, use the zipper foot to sew the stitched piece and the back together, leaving the bottom edges open. Trim the seam, clip curves, and turn right side out. Press the bottom edges under ½". Stuff firmly with fiberfill to within 1½" of the bottom. Fill the plastic bag with enough plastic pellets to equal a 2"-diameter ball. Close the bag with the rubber band, forcing out as much air as possible. Insert the bag of pellets into the bottom of the bag, adding fiberfill as necessary to fill the doll firmly.

Press the edges of the base under ½". Center the base on the body and slip-stitch them together, tucking fiberfill inside the doll as needed.

Red Nutcracker

Anchor		DMC
002	•	000 White
403	■	310 Black
9046	◉	321 Christmas red
9575	▽	353 Dark peach
133	▲	796 Royal blue
137	+	798 Delft blue
897	◆	902 Deep garnet
1012	–	948 Light peach
1013	○	3778 Terra-cotta
1098	✕	3801 Watermelon
	✳	002 Kreinik gold #8 fine braid

HALF CROSS-STITCH
☑ W88 Rainbow Gallery Whisper

BACKSTITCH
002 Kreinik gold #8 fine braid –
jacket and hat trim (1X)
403 ╱ 310 Black – all other stitches (2X)

FRENCH KNOT
○ 002 Kreinik gold #8 fine braid –
coat buttons (1X)

Stitch count: 67 high x 25 wide

Finished design sizes:
11-count fabric – 6 x 2¼ inches
14-count fabric – 4¾ x 1¾ inches
16-count fabric – 4⅛ x 1½ inches

Gold Nutcracker

Anchor		DMC
002	•	000 White
403	■	310 Black
218	▲	319 Dark pistachio
9575	▽	353 Dark peach
217	+	367 Medium pistachio
897	◆	902 Deep garnet
1012	–	948 Light peach
1013	○	3778 Terra-cotta
306	◉	3820 Dark straw
891	✕	3822 Light straw
	✳	002 Kreinik gold #8 fine braid

HALF CROSS-STITCH
☑ W88 Rainbow Gallery Whisper

BACKSTITCH
002 Kreinik gold #8 fine braid –
jacket and hat trim (1X)
403 ╱ 310 Black – all other stitches (2X)

FRENCH KNOT
○ 002 Kreinik gold #8 fine braid –
coat buttons (1X)

Nutcracker

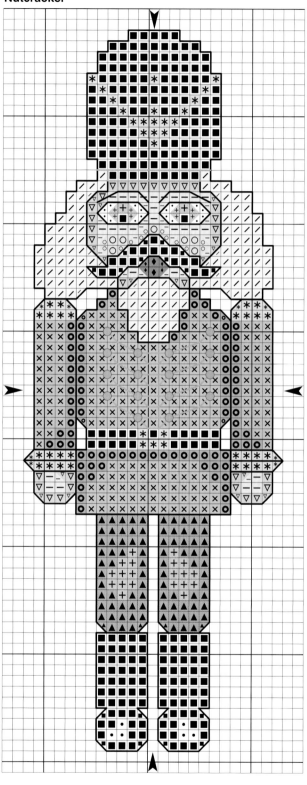

Tree

Trimmings

Looking for the ultimate Christmas tree theme? How about handmade? As long as your tree is decorated with the things you love, it's perfect. For additions to your holiday evergreen this year, look to the following pages. They're filled with all styles of ornaments and a sprightly tree skirt.

Christmas goes contemporary for these tiny pillow trims. *Exquisitely stitched one-over-one on 32-count fabric, the design is shown here in two colorways. If you prefer, work the stitches over two threads of fabric and finish the stitched design as a throw pillow or a holiday tote with sashing strips and a handle.*

Project instructions begin on page 112.
Design: Ruth Sparrow of Twisted Threads. Photographs: Marcia Cameron

With rings on his fingers and bells on his toes, this imp *gives a jingle wherever he goes. Designed as a perforated-paper cutout, the ornament gets a double backing of stiff green and white felt. This extra firmness lets you perch it over a branch of your tree, or place it—front and center—in a festive tabletop display.*

Project instructions begin on page 114.
Design: Barbara Sestok. Photograph: Marcia Cameron

Gingerbread, candy, and sprinkles abound in this taste treat of
Christmas confections. The tree skirt serves up a platter of cross-stitched gingerbread
and sugar cookies with a toss of button "taffy" thrown in for good measure. The
whole thing begins with a prefinished 28-count Silvretta tree skirt, so there's
minimal finishing. Take one, or both, of the gingerbread kids to a new dimension
as chubby pillow decor, opposite. Thanks to beads and a big shank button, this
doll gets covered in colored sprinkles and silver dragées and wears a jellybean
nose. To thoroughly savor this sweet idea, scatter heart morsels all over your tree
and use them as package tie-ons, too!

Project instructions begin on page 116.
Design: Barbara Sestok. Photographs: Perry Struse and Marcia Cameron

A braided-hair angel comes down to earth in this oh-so-quaint and country version. Stitched on Aida cloth, she has all the easygoing elements of a provincial lass—from her calico dress and petticoat to the checkerboard heart and button-trim kitty. It's her heavenly blue perforated paper wings that make her a cherubic ornament!

Project instructions begin on page 120.
Design: Diane Arthurs. Photograph: Scott Little

Ring-a-ling, hear them ring—Christmas bells chime their appeal all over these glimmering holiday ornaments. Finished as tiny linen bags, the gold-and-red duo jingles with Christmas goodies for little fingers to find. The same pair, cast in silver and blue on Aida cloth, take a turn as diagonally set squares. Braid and matching bells set them off to perfection.

Project instructions begin on page 122.
Design: Ursula Michael. Photographs: Perry Struse and Marcia Cameron

stitches

Center and stitch the chart on the fabric. Use one ply of floss to work the stitches over one thread of the fabric unless otherwise specified. Press the stitched piece from the back.

Assembly

Centering the design, trim the finished stitched piece to a 3×4" rectangle. Baste the fleece to the wrong side of the stitched piece ¼" from the raw edges.

From the coordinating cotton fabric, cut a 3×4" rectangle for back, a 1×13" bias hanging strip, and enough 1¼"-wide bias strips to make 18" of piping.

If necessary, sew the short ends of the piping strips together to make one long strip. Center the cording lengthwise on the wrong side of the piping strip. Fold the fabric around the cording with the long edges together. Use a zipper foot to sew through both layers close to the cording. Baste the piping to the front of the stitched piece with the raw edges even.

For the hanger, fold the 1×13" bias strip in half; sew a scant ¼" from the long edge. Turn the strip right side out. Fold the strip in half to form a loop. Sew the loop ends to the top center of the ornament back with the raw edges even.

Sew the ornament front and back together with right sides facing, slightly rounding the corners and leaving an opening for turning. Trim the seams, clip the corners, and turn right side out. Press. Stuff the ornament firmly with polyester fiberfill and slip-stitch the opening closed. Tie a knot in the hanger about 2½" from the fold.

For the twisted cord bow edging, cut two 78" lengths each of Christmas red (DMC 321) or violet (DMC 550), dark Christmas green (DMC 699) or pistachio (DMC 367), and white (DMC 000) floss. Combine the cut lengths into a single strand. Secure one end of the joined strands and twist until tightly wound. Holding the ends, fold the strand in half as the two halves twist around each other. Make a knot 1" from each end, then cut the folded end to fringe. Beginning at the top right corner of the ornament with the center of the twisted cord, tack the twisted cord to the inside edge of the piping. Tie the cord into a bow at the bottom right corner of the ornament.

Ho Ho Ho Ornament

supplies

8" square piece of 32-count antique ivory linen
Cotton embroidery floss
3×4" piece of fleece
¼ yard of coordinating cotton fabric
½ yard of ⅛"-diameter cording
Matching sewing thread
Polyester fiberfill

Muted Option

Anchor		DMC	
002	•	000	White
217	×	367	Pistachio
102	●	550	Violet
043	♡	815	Garnet

Stitch count: 50 high x 70 wide

Finished design sizes:
(over one thread)
32-count fabric – 1½ x 2⅛ inches
36-count fabric – 1⅓ x 2 inches
28-count fabric – 1¾ x 2½ inches

Bright Option

Anchor		DMC	
002	•	000	White
9046	♡	321	Christmas red
382	●	3371	Black-brown
923	×	3818	Emerald

Stitch count: 50 high x 70 wide

Finished design sizes:
(over two threads)
32-count fabric – 3⅛ x 4⅜ inches
36-count fabric – 2¾ x 3⅞ inches
28-count fabric – 3½ x 5 inches

Ho Ho Ho Ornament

Climbing Elf Ornament

supplies
5×6" piece of 14-count cream perforated paper
Cotton embroidery floss
Kreinik gold (002) #16 medium braid and #8 fine braid
Mill Hill Rondele beads
5×6" piece each of white and green stiffened felt
Crafts glue
3—6mm gold jingle bells
6" length of narrow gold cord

stitches
Center and stitch the chart on the perforated paper. Use two plies of floss to work the stitches unless otherwise specified. For the string of lights, thread a large-eye tapestry needle with gold medium braid. Insert the needle into the back of the perforated paper at the position marked on the chart. Bring the medium braid across the front of the ornament to the next position marked on the chart. Use the fine braid to work couching stitches over the medium braid and to attach the beads as indicated on the chart. Use two plies of light Christmas green (DMC 702) floss to attach the jingle bells.

assembly
Trim the stitched piece one square beyond the stitched area of the design, allowing extra paper around the bells and the string of lights. Center the stitched piece on the white felt and glue in place. Trim away the excess white felt ⅛" beyond the perforated paper. For the hanger, glue the ends of the gold cord to the top center on the back of the white felt shape. Center and glue the white felt shape on the green felt. Trim the excess green felt ⅛" beyond the white felt.

Climbing Elf Ornament

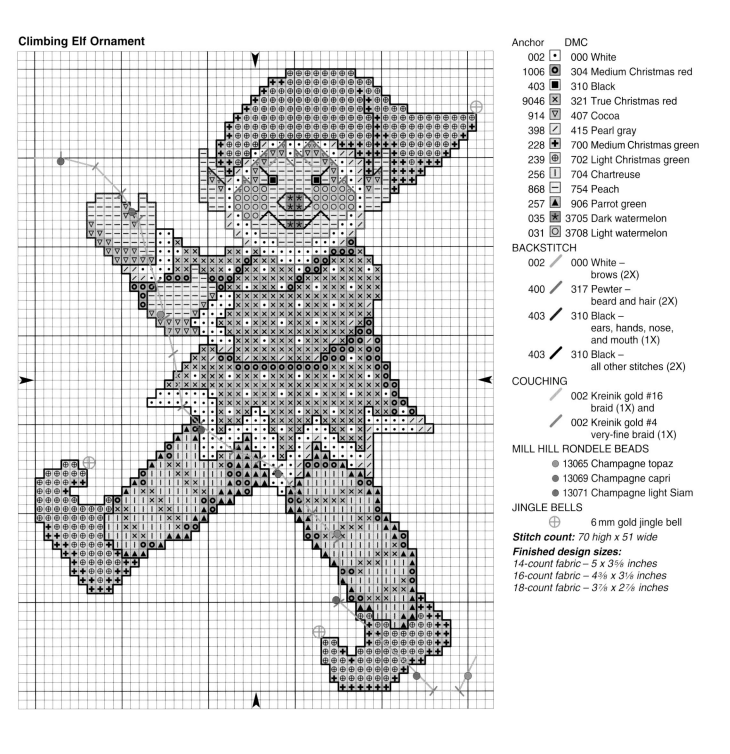

Anchor		DMC	
002	·	000	White
1006	◎	304	Medium Christmas red
403	■	310	Black
9046	×	321	True Christmas red
914	▽	407	Cocoa
398	∕	415	Pearl gray
228	✚	700	Medium Christmas green
239	⊕	702	Light Christmas green
256		704	Chartreuse
868	–	754	Peach
257	▲	906	Parrot green
035	✳	3705	Dark watermelon
031	◙	3708	Light watermelon

BACKSTITCH

002	∕	000	White – brows (2X)
400	∕	317	Pewter – beard and hair (2X)
403	∕	310	Black – ears, hands, nose, and mouth (1X)
403	∕	310	Black – all other stitches (2X)

COUCHING

	∕	002 Kreinik gold #16 braid (1X) and
	∕	002 Kreinik gold #4 very-fine braid (1X)

MILL HILL RONDELE BEADS

	●	13065 Champagne topaz
	●	13069 Champagne capri
	●	13071 Champagne light Siam

JINGLE BELLS

	⊕	6 mm gold jingle bell

Stitch count: 70 high x 51 wide

Finished design sizes:
14-count fabric – 5 x 3⅝ inches
16-count fabric – 4⅜ x 3⅛ inches
18-count fabric – 3⅞ x 2⅞ inches

edges together. Use a zipper foot to sew through both layers close to the cording. Sew the piping around the perimeter of the doll shape with the raw edges facing out and the seam line of the piping atop the basting stitches on the stitched piece.

With right sides together, center the stitched piece on the 12×15" back piece; pin. Sew the stitched piece to the back atop the basting line, leaving an opening along the top edge of one arm for turning. Trim the seam allowances to ¼". Clip curves; turn right side out. Stuff the doll firmly with polyester fiberfill and slip-stitch the opening closed. Sew the red button nose to the center of the face as indicated.

Heart Gift Tags
The chart and key are on pages 118–119.

supplies
For each gift tag
4" square of 14-count tan perforated paper
Cotton embroidery floss
4mm E beads: 11 green, 6 orange, 13 red, and 11 yellow
24—4mm round silver-plated beads
White embossed dot paper
Crafts glue
Gold metallic pen

stitches
Center and stitch a heart from the Gingerbread Tree Skirt chart on the perforated paper, eliminating the backstitching. Use two plies of floss to work the stitches. Use two plies of matching floss to attach the beads.

assembly
Trim the stitched piece one square beyond the stitching. From the white embossed paper, cut a 2¼×3½" rectangle. Referring to the photograph

Gingerbread Doll
The chart and key are on pages 118–119.

supplies
15×18" piece of 10-count sand Tula fabric
Cotton embroidery floss
1 additional skein each of white (DMC 000) and light Christmas green (DMC 702)
4mm E beads: 27 red, 24 yellow, and 23 each of green and orange
32—4mm silver-plated beads
⅜ yard of 44"-wide tan print fabric
12×15" piece of fleece
Tan sewing thread
1⅜ yard of ⅛"-diameter cording
Polyester fiberfill
1-9/16"-diameter red shank button

stitches
Center and stitch the boy or girl from the Gingerbread Tree Skirt chart onto the Tula fabric. Use four plies of floss to work the stitches over one square unless otherwise specified. Use two plies of matching floss to attach the beads. Press the stitched piece from the back.

assembly
Center the stitched piece right side up on the fleece; pin. For the finished shape of the doll, machine-baste ¼" to ½" beyond the outermost stitches, simplifying the shape and keeping the curves smooth.

From the tan fabric, cut a 12×15" piece for the back and enough 1¼"-wide bias strips to make 48" of piping.

Sew the short ends of the piping strips together to make one long strip. Center the cording lengthwise on the wrong side of the piping strip. Fold the fabric around the cording with the long *opposite below,* glue the heart onto the embossed paper. Use the gold metallic pen to personalize the gift tag.

Gingerbread Tree Skirt
The chart and key are on pages 118–119.

supplies
Purchased 58"-diameter 28-count gold-and-cream Silvretta tree skirt
Cotton embroidery floss
1 additional skein *each* of white (DMC 000), light Christmas green (DMC 702), and cyclamen (DMC 3806)
2 additional skeins of dark golden brown (DMC 3826)
4mm E beads: red, yellow, green, and orange
4mm round silver-plated beads
2—6mm pearl beads
2—9/16"-diameter red shank buttons
3—7/16"-diameter red shank buttons
5¾ yards of ⅜"-wide pink-and-white polka-dot grosgrain ribbon
Pink sewing thread
40—¾"-diameter white shank buttons
Acrylic paint: bright green, bright orange, bright pink, and bright yellow
Paintbrush
Ultra fine clear glitter
2½ yards of 2"-wide white sparkling sheer wire-edged ribbon

stitches
To position the designs on the tree skirt, refer to the diagram on *page 119.* Measure up from the outer edge of the lace and out from the vertical center of the skirt. Use three plies of floss to work the stitches over two threads of the fabric unless otherwise specified in the key.

Find the vertical center of the heart chart and the tree skirt. For the center heart, measure up 5½" along the vertical center of the skirt; begin stitching the bottom of the heart there. For the gingerbread boy and girl, measure up 3½", then 2¾" out from the center; begin stitching the toe of the boot or shoe there. For the left and right hearts, measure up 6", then 11½" out from the

center; begin stitching the bottom of the heart there.

Use two plies of matching floss to attach the beads. For the nose, sew a 9/16"-diameter red button to the center of each face as indicated. Sew the 7/16"-diameter red buttons below the boy's neck for holly berries.

assembly
Position the grosgrain ribbon on the lace of the tree skirt, covering the gold band. Edge-stitch the ribbon in place along both long edges.

To make the candies, divide the white buttons into four groups. Paint one group green. While the paint is wet, lightly sprinkle glitter on the top of each button; let the paint dry. Repeat for the remaining button groups, using orange, pink, and yellow paints.

Cut a 2" length of wire-edged ribbon for each button. Center a painted button, glitter side down, on one piece of ribbon. Fold the cut edges of the ribbon *continued*

around the button, forming a tube with the wire edges on the ends. Thread a needle with two plies of white floss; knot one end. On the shank side of the button, take a tiny stitch in the ribbon close to the button. Wrap the floss around the ribbon and take a second tiny stitch close to the first stitch. Pull the floss tightly, gathering the ribbon. Wrap the floss around the ribbon once more and secure with two or three stitches. Repeat for the opposite side of the button.

Lay the tree skirt out on a flat surface and arrange the candies on the skirt. Sew the candies to the skirt through the shank of the button.

Anchor		DMC
002	·	000 White
110	⊠	208 Lavender
075	/	604 Cranberry
228	▲	700 Medium Christmas green
239	✕	702 Light Christmas green
255	▽	907 Parrot green
381	❋	938 Coffee brown
297	✳	973 Canary
355	◗	975 Deep golden brown
329	−	3340 Melon
060	○	3806 Cyclamen
1048	+	3826 Dark golden brown
305	◨	3852 Straw

BACKSTITCH (1X)
002		000 White – vest
403	/	310 Black – all other stitches

Anchor		DMC

BACKSTITCH (1X)
235	/	318 Steel – icing shadow
9046	/	321 Christmas red – gingerbread mouths

LAZY DAISY (1X)
002		000 White – Gingerbread man's hair

ATTACHMENTS
✕	5406 Pearl 6 mm bead – vest
○	6304 Silver-tone 4 mm bead
○	8022 Green 4 mm bead
●	8022 Orange 4 mm bead
●	8022 Red 4 mm bead
○	8022 Yellow 4 mm bead
✕	7⁄16" red shank button – holly berries
✕	9⁄16" red shank button – gingerbread noses

Gingerbread Tree Skirt

Gingerbread Boy stitch count:
121 high x 251 wide

Gingerbread Boy finished design sizes:
28-count fabric – 8⅝ x 6½ inches
32-count fabric – 7½ x 5⅝ inches
36-count fabric – 6¾ x 5 inches

Gingerbread Girl stitch count:
120 high x 91 wide

Gingerbread Girl finished design sizes:
28-count fabric – 8½ x 6½ inches
32-count fabric – 7½ x 5⅝ inches
36-count fabric – 6⅔ x 5 inches

Heart stitch count: *39 high x 39 wide*

Heart finished design sizes:
28-count fabric – 2¾ x 2¾ inches
32-count fabric – 2⅜ x 2⅜ inches
36-count fabric – 2⅛ x 2⅛ inches

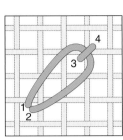

Lazy Daisy Stitch

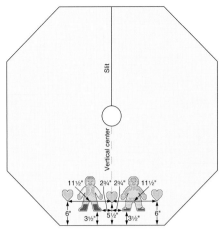

Gingerbread Tree Skirt Diagram

Floss-Hair Angel

supplies

8" square of 14-count light oatmeal
  Fiddler's Lite Aida cloth
4×8" piece of 14-count brown
  perforated paper
Cotton embroidery floss
Just My Imagination ⅞" cat button
Yarn needle
Fusible interfacing
Tracing paper
8" square *each* of medium-weight
  cardboard and felt
Crafts glue

stitches

Center and stitch the angel on the Aida
cloth. Use three plies of floss to work the
stitches over one square unless otherwise
specified. Work the French knots using
two plies of floss wrapped twice around.

For the hair, cut eight 9" lengths of
six-ply hazel (DMC 869) floss. Knot

one end of one strand. Holding the knot
securely, twist the strand until it begins to
kink. Carefully fold the strand in half and
allow it to twist on itself. Trim away the
first knot and tie the two ends together.
Thread the folded end into the yarn
needle. From the back of the fabric, pull
the twisted strand through at the top of
the angel's head, just beyond the
backstitches. Repeat with the remaining
8" strands of floss. Press the stitched
piece facedown on a padded surface.

Center and stitch the wings on the
perforated paper. Use three plies of floss
to work the stitches over one square
unless otherwise specified.

assembly

Center and fuse the interfacing to the
back of the stitched Aida cloth following
manufacturer's instructions. Cut out the
the angel ⅝" beyond the stitching, being
careful not to cut the hair.

To make a pattern, place tracing
paper over the stitched fabric and trace
around the design about 1/16" beyond the
backstitches, smoothing the curves; cut
out. Use the paper pattern to cut one
each from cardboard and felt.

Center the stitched piece on the
cardboard. Wrap excess fabric to the
back and glue. For the hanger, cut two
19" stands of hazel six-ply floss; combine
the strands and fold in half. Knot the
ends and twist as directed for the hair.
Bring the knotted and the folded ends
together to form a loop. Wrap a single
ply of floss around the two ends and
secure. Then trim away the knot. Glue
the wrapped end to the back of the
angel's head. Glue the felt shape to the
back of the angel.

Cut out the angel wings one square
beyond the stitching. Glue to the back
of the angel.

Floss-Hair Angel Wings

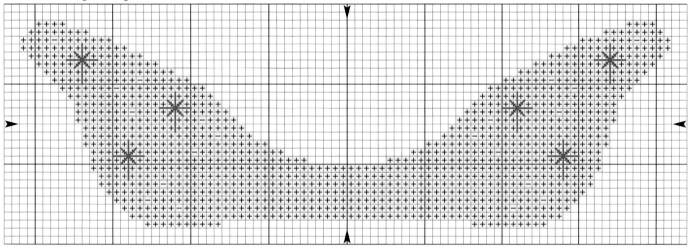

Anchor		DMC
1005	⊞	498 Christmas red
890	◉	680 Old gold
375	◆	869 Hazel
1044	✳	895 Hunter green
897	♥	902 Garnet
837	⊞	927 Gray-blue
1034	▣	931 Medium antique blue
4146	•	950 Rose-beige
074	♡	3354 Dusty rose
305	⊟	3821 Straw

BACKSTITCH

897	╱	902 Garnet – dress (1X), heart (2X)
1035	╱	930 Dark antique blue – wings, dress (2X)
382	╱	3371 Black-brown – angel (1X), facial features (2X)

FRENCH KNOT

382	●	3371 Black-brown – flower center

SURFACE ATTACHMENTS

	✕	Cat button – dress

Angel stitch count: *56 high x 56 wide*

Angel finished design sizes:
14-count fabric – 4 x 4 inches
16-count fabric – 3½ x 3½ inches
18-count fabric – 3¼ x 3¼ inches

Wing stitch count: *26 high x 84 wide*

Wing finished design sizes:
14-count fabric – 1⅞ x 6 inches
16-count fabric – 1⅝ x 5¼ inches
18-count fabric – 1½ x 4⅔ inches

Floss-Hair Angel

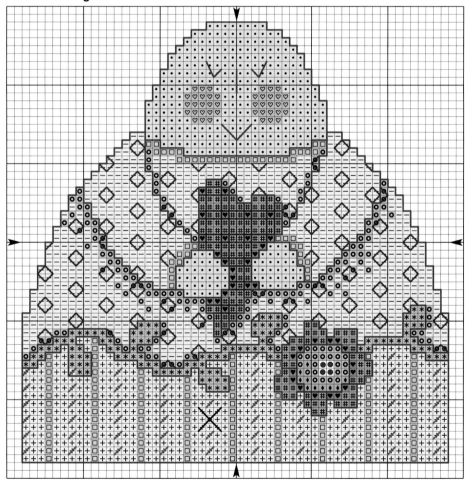

press. Hand-sew the twisted cord to the sides of the ornament.

Silver Bells Ornaments

supplies
For each ornament
9" square piece of 14-count platinum Aida cloth
Cotton embroidery floss
3½" square *each* of self-stick mounting board with foam and light gray felt
½ yard of ⅜"-wide metallic silver trim
8" length of ⅛"-wide metallic silver ribbon
2—¾" silver liberty bells or 18mm silver jingle bells
Kreinik silver (001) ¹⁄₁₆"-wide ribbon
Crafts glue

stitches
Center and stitch the chart on the Aida cloth. Use three plies of floss to work the stitches over one square unless otherwise specified. Press the stitched piece from the back.

Golden Bells Ornaments

supplies
For each ornament
9" square piece of 27-count Northern Cross tea-color linen
Cotton embroidery floss
1 additional skein *each* of rose (DMC 309), light garnet (DMC 816), and medium rose-pink (DMC 962)
6×18" piece of coordinating print cotton fabric
6" square of muslin
Matching sewing thread

stitches
Center and stitch the chart on the linen. Use three plies of floss to work the stitches over two threads of the fabric unless otherwise specified. Press the stitched piece from the back.

assembly
Trim the finished stitched piece ¾" beyond the green border of the design. Use the trimmed piece as a pattern to cut a back and two lining pieces from the coordinating print fabric and one underlining from the muslin.

For the twisted cord, cut three 54" strands each of rose (DMC 309), light garnet (DMC 816), and medium

rose-pink (DMC 962) floss. Combine the cut lengths into a single strand and tie a knot in each end. Secure one knot to a stationary object and twist the opposite end until the floss is very tightly twisted and begins to kink. Holding the ends, fold the strand in half and allow the two halves to twist around each other. Make another knot to secure the knotted ends together.

Center the muslin on the back of the stitched piece; baste ¼" from the edges. Position the ends of the twisted cord at the bottom corners of the ornament front about ⅜" from the bottom edge. Adjust the cord ends for the length of hanger you desire; sew ends to ornament front.

Sew the ornament front and back together along the sides and bottom using ¼" seams, leaving the top edge open and taking care to catch only the ends of the twisted cord. Trim the excess cord and clip the corners; turn right side out and press. Sew the lining pieces together in the same manner (omitting the twisted cord). Leave an opening in one side for turning, but *do not* turn.

Slip the ornament inside the lining with the seams matching and raw edges even. Sew around the top edges; turn right side out through the opening in the lining. Slip-stitch the opening closed. Tuck the lining into the ornament and

assembly

Peel the protective paper from the mounting board. Center the foam side on the back of the stitched piece and press to stick. Trim the excess fabric ½" beyond the edge of the board. Fold the edge of the fabric to the back and glue in place.

Position and glue the trim around the edge of the ornament, overlapping the ends at the bottom center. Trim the excess trim and glue the ends to the ornament back. For the hanger, fold the ⅛" ribbon in half to form a loop. Glue the ends to the top center back of the ornament. Cut two 5" lengths of ⅟₁₆"-wide ribbon and thread a bell on each length. Bring the ribbon ends together and adjust so the bells hang at slightly different heights. Tie a knot in the ribbons about ½" from the bells. Glue the knot to the bottom center back of the ornament; trim the excess ribbon. Glue the felt to the ornament back.

Golden Bells Ornaments

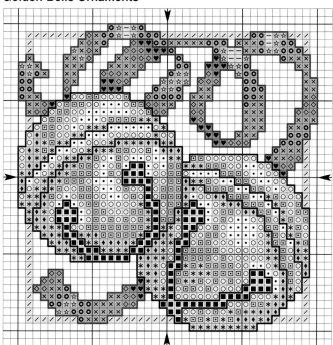

Anchor		DMC
1006	✗	304 Christmas red
042	◉	309 Rose
923	╱	699 Christmas green
891	✳	729 Medium old gold
045	♥	814 Dark garnet
1005	◇	816 Light garnet
075	☆	962 Medium rose-pink
382	■	3371 Black-brown
025	−	3716 Light rose-pink
306	▣	3820 Dark straw
305	○	3821 True straw
891	•	3822 Light straw
901	◆	3829 Deep old gold

BACKSTITCH (1X)

045	╱	814 Dark garnet – ribbon
382	╱	3371 Black-brown – jingle bells

Stitch count: *40 high x 40 wide*
Finished design sizes:
28-count fabric – 2⅞ x 2⅞ inches
32-count fabric – 2½ x 2½ inches
36-count fabric – 2¼ x 2¼ inches

Silver Bells Ornaments

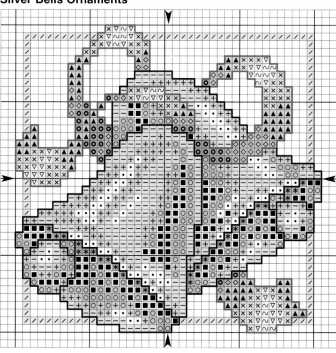

Anchor		DMC
002	•	000 White
400	✳	317 Pewter
399	○	318 Light steel
235	■	414 Dark steel
398	+	415 Light pearl gray
923	╱	699 Christmas green
234	−	762 Pale pearl gray
132	◇	797 Light royal blue
137	▲	798 Dark Delft blue
136	✗	799 Medium Delft blue
144	∼	800 Pale Delft blue
130	▽	809 True Delft blue
134	◉	820 Dark royal blue

BACKSTITCH (1X)

152	╱	939 Navy – ribbon
236	╱	3799 Charcoal – bells

Stitch count: *40 high x 41 wide*
Finished design sizes:
14-count fabric – 2⅞ x 3 inches
16-count fabric – 2½ x 2½ inches
18-count fabric – 2¼ x 2¼ inches

Cross-Stitch Basics

getting started

The written instructions for each project indicate where to begin stitching. For most projects the starting point is at the center. Every chart has arrows that indicate the horizontal and vertical centers. With your finger, trace along the grid to the point where the two centers meet. Compare a symbol at the center of the chart to the key and choose which floss color to stitch first. To find the center of the fabric, fold it into quarters and finger-crease or baste along the folds with a single ply of contrasting floss.

Cut the floss into 15" lengths, and separate all six plies. Recombine the plies as indicated in the project instructions, and thread them into a blunt-tip needle.

basic cross-stitch

Make one cross-stitch for each symbol on the chart. For horizontal rows, stitch the first diagonal of each stitch in the row. Work back across the row, completing each stitch. On most linen and even-weave fabrics, work the stitches over two threads as shown in the diagram *below*. For Aida cloth, each stitch fills one square.

You also can work cross-stitches in the reverse direction. Remember to embroider the stitches uniformly—that is, always work the top half of each stitch in the same direction.

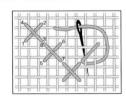

Cross-stitch worked singly

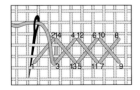

Cross-stitch worked in rows

to secure thread at the beginning

The most common way to secure the beginning tail of the thread is to hold it under the first four or five stitches.

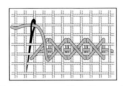

Stitching over the thread tail

To secure the thread with a waste knot, thread the needle and knot the end of the thread. Insert the needle from the right side of fabric, about 4 inches away from the first stitch. Bring the needle up through the fabric, and work the first series of stitches. When finished, clip the knot on the right side. Rethread the needle with excess floss and push the needle through to the stitches on the wrong side of the fabric.

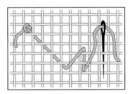

Waste knot

When working with two, four, or six plies of floss, use a loop knot. Cut half as many plies of thread, making each one twice as long. Recombine the plies, fold the strand in half, and thread all of the ends into the needle. Work the first diagonal of the first stitch, and slip the needle through the loop formed by folding the thread.

Loop knot

to secure thread at the end

To finish, slip the threaded needle under previously stitched threads on the wrong side of the fabric for four or five stitches, weaving the thread back and forth a few times. Clip the thread.

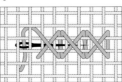

Securing thread at the end

quarter and three-quarter cross-stitches

To obtain rounded shapes in a design, use quarter and three-quarter cross-stitches. On linen and even-weave fabrics, a quarter cross-stitch will extend from the corner to the center intersection of the threads. To make quarter cross-stitches on Aida cloth, estimate the center of the square. Three-quarter cross-stitches combine a quarter cross-stitch with a half cross-stitch. Both stitches may slant in any direction.

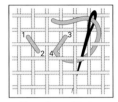

Quarter stitches

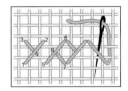

Three-quarter stitches

algerian eyelet

The key to making this spoked stitch with its center hole is to work from the outside in. Bring the needle from the back to the front at an outside edge of the stitch, then push it to the back at the at the midpoint of the stitch, pulling the thread firmly and gently. As you work successive spokes, an opening will appear in the middle.

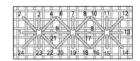

Algerian eyelets in a row

backstitches

Backstitches define and outline the shapes of a design. For most projects, backstitches require only one ply of

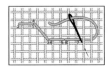

Backstitches

floss. On the color key, (2X) indicates two plies of floss, (3X) indicates three plies, etc.

chain stitch

Bring the needle to the front of the fabric, and return to the back through the same hole, forming a loop. Slide the tip of the needle under two or more threads and bring it to the front of the fabric. Slip the loop under the needle tip. Pull gently until the loop lies smoothly on the fabric. Pass the needle to the back, forming the loop of the second stitch of the chain.

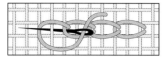

Chain stitches

couching

Use two needles to work a line of couching. Bring the heavier couched thread through the fabric at the beginning of the line designated on the chart and to the back at the end. Roughly align it in the position indicated on the chart. Bring the lighter couching thread through the fabric four threads (unless otherwise specified on chart) beyond the entry point of the couched thread, over it, and to the back in the next hole. Move four threads along the line of the couched thread, and repeat the couching. Continue along the entire length of the couched thread.

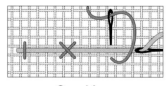

Couching

cross-stitches with beads

Beads may be attached by working the first half of each cross-stitch and attaching a bead on the return stitch. To ensure that beads stand up straight, work with two plies of floss and add the bead to the first half stitch. As you work the second diagonal, split the plies so one ply lies on each side of the bead.

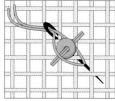

Securing a bead

french knot

Bring the threaded needle through the fabric, and wrap the floss around the needle as shown. Tighten the twists, and return the needle through the fabric in the same place. The floss will slide through the wrapped thread to make the knot.

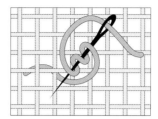

French knot

half cross-stitches

A half cross-stitch is a single diagonal or half a cross-stitch. They usually are listed under a separate heading in the color key and are indicated on the chart by a diagonal colored line.

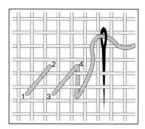

Half cross-stitch

lazy-daisy stitch

Bring the needle to the front of the fabric, and return to the back through the same hole, forming a loop. Slide the tip of the needle under two or more threads, then bring it to the front of the fabric. Slip the loop under the needle tip. Pull gently until the loop lies smoothly on the fabric. Push the needle to the back, forming a tack stitch over the end of the loop.

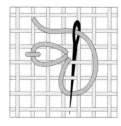

Lazy-daisy stitch

running stitch

Running stitches work up fast and add design definition. They are usually equal in length, although uneven stitches create a novelty effect.

Running stitches

satin stitch

This smooth-surface stitch may be worked over a few or many threads. Bring up the needle up through the first hole. Count threads along a straight line, and return to the back of the fabric. For the second stitch, bring up the needle through the hole immediately next to the first stitch.

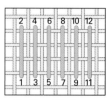

Satin stitches

smyrna cross-stitch

A Smyrna cross-stitch consists of an X-shape stitch topped by a straight horizontal stitch and a straight-vertical stitch. It's often worked over four, six, eight, or more threads.

Smyrna cross stitch

straight stitches

The simplest of all stitches, straight stitches often are used for sun rays, whiskers, and other simple accents.

Straight stitches

changing materials

Many stitchers work cross-stitch designs using fabrics and threads other than those specified in the projects. Use this helpful information to complete the projects in this book while adapting them to your own preferences.

Before you begin a project on a fabric other than that specified, stitch a small
continued

sample. Be sure you're happy with the amount of detail on the new fabric and the way the thread covers it. Also note whether the needle slips smoothly through the fabric.

cross-stitch fabrics

Work counted cross-stitch on any fabric that lets you make consistently sized, even stitches. Many fabrics marketed specifically for cross-stitch are interchangeable when the stitch-per-inch counts match. For example, a project that calls for 28-count linen stitched over two threads can easily be worked on 14-count Aida. A higher count fabric will yield a smaller project. When a design is enlarged by working on lower count fabric, some of the detail may be lost. The charts in this book offer conversion information that indicates the size of the design when worked on other fabric counts.

Aida cloth is the most popular cross-stitch fabric. The threads are woven in groups separated by tiny spaces to create a pattern of squares across the surface of the fabric so a beginning stitcher can easily see where to place the cross-stitches. Measure Aida cloth by the number of squares per inch; for example, 14-count Aida cloth has 14 squares per inch. Look for Aida cloth in 6, 8, 11, 14, 16, and 18 thread counts. You'll find 14-count Aida cloth in more than 60 colors. For beginners, white Aida cloth is available with a removable grid of pre-basted threads.

Experienced stitchers consider linen the standard of excellence in cross-stitch fabrics. The threads used to weave linen vary in thickness, giving the fabric a slightly irregular surface. Measure thread count by the number of threads per inch. Because most designs are worked over two threads, 28-count linen usually yields 14 stitches per inch. Linens are made in counts from 14 (seven stitches per inch) to 45.

The market for specialty fabrics for counted cross-stitch continues to grow with the popularity of the craft. These fabrics are referred to as even-weave fabrics because they're woven from threads with a consistent diameter, although some have a homespun look. Count most even-weaves like linen—by the number of threads per inch—and stitch over two threads.

Use Hardanger fabric for very fine counted cross-stitch. The traditional fabric for Norwegian embroidery of the same name has an over-two, under-two weave that produces 22 small squares per inch.

Use waste canvas to cross-stitch on clothing and fabrics that aren't otherwise suitable for stitching. The canvas marks the squares and is designed to ravel when dampened after stitching is complete. It ranges in count from 6½ to 20 stitches per inch.

Cross-stitch charts can be worked 32- or 40-count silk gauze, 14-count perforated paper, 6- to 24-count needlepoint canvas, or plastic canvas. These materials make no provision for fractional (quarter and three-quarter) stitches, so choose a chart with whole stitches only.

threads for stitching

Most types of commercially available embroidery thread are adaptable for counted cross-stitch projects.

Six-ply cotton embroidery floss has the widest range of colors, including variegated colors. It separates easily into single or multiple plies for stitching. The instructions with each project in this book list how many plies to use. If you select a different-count fabric than the one specified, use the chart on this page as a guide, and experiment on a scrap of the fabric until you achieve the desired effect. A greater number of plies will result in a dense or heavily textured piece; a smaller number of plies will create a lightweight or delicate texture.

Rayon and silk floss are similar in weight to six-ply cotton embroidery floss but with a higher sheen. Both can be interchanged with cotton floss, one ply for one ply. Because they have a "slicker" texture, you may find them more difficult to use.

Pearl cotton is available in four sizes: #3, #5, #8, and #12 (#3 is heavy; #12 is fine). It has an obvious twist and a high sheen.

Flower thread is a matte-finish cotton thread. Substitute one strand of flower thread for two plies of floss.

A product growing in popularity is overdyed thread. Most colors have an irregularly variegated, one-of-a-kind appearance. Cotton floss, silk floss, flower thread, and pearl cotton are all available in this form. All produce a soft, shaded appearance without changing thread colors. The color changes can be enhanced by working each stitch individually.

Specialty threads add a distinctive look to cross-stitch work. They range in weight from hair-fine blending filament, usually used with floss, to ⅛-inch-wide ribbon. Specialty threads include numerous metallic threads, richly colored and textured threads, and fun-to-stitch glow-in-the-dark threads.

needle types

Blunt-tip needles work best on most cross-stitch fabrics because they slide through the holes and between threads without splitting or snagging the fibers. A large-eyed needle accommodates most threads. Some companies sell such needles labeled "cross-stitch," but they're identical to tapestry needles—blunt tipped and large eyed. Use the chart *below* to guide you to the right needle size for common fabrics.

An exception to the blunt-tip needle is waste canvas. Since it's usually basted to a tightly woven fabric, a sharp embroidery needle is required to penetrate the fabric beneath.

Seed beads require very fine needles that will slide through the holes. Two readily available options are a #8 quilting needle, which is short with a tiny eye, and a long beading needle, which has a longer eye.

Fabric/Needles/Floss

Fabric	Tapestry-Needle Size	Number of Plies
11-Count	24	Three
14-Count	24-26	Two
18-Count	26	Two
22-Count	26	One

Index

Sources

Many of the materials and items used in this book are available at crafts and needlework stores. For more information, write or call the manufacturers listed below.

Christmas Carols

Lo, How a Rose, *pages 8–9:* Belfast linen—Wichelt Imports, Inc. or Zweigart. Perforated paper—Yarn Tree Designs. Crystal Treasures and Celeste banding—Mill Hill.

I Saw Three Ships, *pages 10–11:* Dusty miller Aida cloth—Wichelt Imports, Inc. Rustico Aida cloth—Zweigart. Square oak box—Sudberry House, Box 895, Old Lyme, CT 06371

Frosty the Snowman, *page 11:* Jobelan fabric—Wichelt Imports, Inc.

It's Beginning to Look Like Christmas, *page 12:* Snowflakes—Mill Hill. Ceramic star buttons—DeCuyper Trading Co. 10226 S. Braden Ave. Tulsa, OK 74137; Papieretto novelty thread—Ogier Trading Co. P. O. Box 686, 2385 Carlos St., Suite D, Moss Beach, CA 94038-0686. ¼"-diameter buttons—JHB International, Inc.; www.buttons.com; 303/751-8100. Doily—Wimpole Street Creations, 419 W 500S, Bountiful, UT 84010; www.barrett-house.com. Frame—ILUVMOO, P.O. Box 153, 202 N. Edison St., Freeburg, IL 62243-0153.

O Little Town of Bethlehem, *pages 12–13:* Jobelan fabric—Wichelt Imports, Inc. Greeting card—Yarn Tree Designs.

Holiday Memories

Christmas Tree Sampler, *pages 26–27:* Perforated paper—Yarn Tree Designs. Banding—Zweigart.

O, Star of Wonder, *pages 28–29:* Sienna linen—Norden Crafts, Ltd. Lambswool linen—Wichelt Imports, Inc.

Antique Candy Tin, *page 30:* Country French latte linen and China pearl Aida—Wichelt Imports, Inc. Papier-mâché box—Decorator & Craft Corp., 428 S. Zelta St., Wichita, KS 67207; 316/685-6265. Silver-and-white Aida cloth—Zweigart. Glass paperweight—Yarn Tree Designs.

Snow Angels, *page 31:* Monet blue linen—Wichelt Imports, Inc. Crown plate frame—Sudberry House.

House Full of Santa

Santa Moon Ornaments, *page 44:* Sky blue linen—Wichelt Imports, Inc. Perforated paper—Yarn Tree Designs.

Folk Art Santa, *page 45:* Beige Aida cloth—Wichelt Imports, Inc. or Zweigart. Buttons, Just Another Button Company.

Bell Pull Santa, *pages 46–47:* Ivory linen—Wichelt Imports, Inc. Clay linen—Norden Crafts, Ltd. Navy Aida cloth—Wichelt Imports, Inc.

Santas on Parade, *pages 48–49:* Heatherfield fabric—Wichelt Imports, Inc. Perforated paper—Yarn Tree Designs. Tula fabric—Wichelt Imports, Inc. or Zweigart.

Santa Towel, *page 50:* Towel—Charles Craft.

Stitched for Giving

Scarf, Hat, and Mitten Patches, *page 64:* Patches—Zweigart.

Holiday Evening Bag, *pages 64–65:* Christmas red Aida cloth—Wichelt Imports, Inc. or Zweigart. Antique blue linen—Wichelt Imports, Inc.

Royal Needle Case, *page 66:* Edinburgh linen—Wichelt Imports, Inc. or Zweigart. Ivory linen—Wichelt Imports, Inc.

Vienna Rose Pillow, *page 67:* Vienna fabric—Zweigart. Stitch & Zip eyeglass case—Alice Peterson Co., 118 Center St., El Segundo, CA 90245.

Work of Mine Book Cover, *page 68:* Cashel linen—Wichelt Imports, Inc. or Zweigart.

Season's Greetings Sampler, *pages 68–69:* Denim bib—Charles Craft. Banding—Zweigart.

Traditions Renewed

Counting the Days, *page 84:* Betsy Ross linen—Wichelt Imports, Inc. Star buttons—Mill Hill. Black buttons—Blumenthal Lansing Co.

Show Towel-Style Stocking, *page 85:* Cashel linen—Wichelt Imports, Inc. or Zweigart.

Gingerbread House Tea Cozy, *page 86:* Coffee bean linen—Wichelt Imports, Inc. Janina fabric—Zweigart. Perforated plastic—Darice Inc., 13000 Darice Parkway, Park 82, Strongsville, OH 44149; www.darice.com. Ribbonfloss—Rhode Island Textile Co., P.O. Box 999, Pawtucket, RI 02862.

Christmas Village Stocking, *page 88:* Spun silver linen—Wichelt Imports, Inc.

Tree Trimmings

Ho Ho Ho Ornament, *page 106:* Antique ivory linen—Wichelt Imports, Inc. or Zweigart.

Climbing Elf Ornament, *page 107:* Perforated paper—Yarn Tree Designs.

Gingerbread Tree Skirt, *pages 108–109:* Silvretta tree skirt—Zweigart. Beads—Sulyn Industries, 11927 W. Sample Rd., Coral Springs, FL 33065. Buttons—Blumenthal Lansing Co. Ribbon—C.M.

Offray & Sons, Inc., Route 24, Box 601, Chester, NJ 07930; 908/879-4700.

Floss-Hair Angel, *page 110:* Fiddler's Lite Aida cloth—Charles Craft. Perforated paper—Yarn Tree Designs.

Golden and Silver Bell Ornaments, *page 111:* Northern Cross linen—Norden Crafts Ltd. Platinum Aida cloth—Wichelt Imports, Inc.

Buttons and Beads

Blumenthal Lansing Co., 1 Palmer Terrace, Carlstadt, NJ 07072.

Just Another Button Co., 116 W. Market St., Troy, IL 62294.

Mill Hill, www.millhillbeads.com, 800/447-1332.

Fabrics

Charles Craft, P.O. Box 1049, Laurinburg, NC 28253; www.charlescraft.com.

Norden Crafts, Ltd., www.nordencrafts.com; 847/891-0770.

Wichelt Imports, Inc., Rte. 1, Stoddard, WI 54658; www.wichelt.com.

Yarn Tree Designs, 117 Alexander St., P.O. Box 724, Ames, IA 50010; www.yarntree.com. 800/247-3952.

Zweigart, 2 Riverview Dr., Somerset, NJ 08873-1139; www.zweigart.com, 732/271-1949.

Threads

Anchor, Consumer Service Dept., P.O. Box 12229, Greenville, SC 29612; www.coatsandclark.com.

DMC, Port Kearney Bldg. 10, South Kearney, NJ 07032-0650; www.dmc-usa.com.

The Gentle Art, 4081 Bremo Recess, New Albany, OH 43054, e-mail: gentleart@aol.com; 614/855-8346, fax 614/855-4298.

Kreinik Manufacturing Co., Inc., 800/537-2166 or Daisy Chain, P.O. Box 1258, Parkersburg, WV 26102; www.kreinik.com, 304/428-9500.

Rainbow Gallery, 7412 Fulton Ave. Ste. 5, North Hollywood, CA 91605; www.rainbowgallery.com.

Weeks Dyeworks, 404 Raleigh St., Fuquay-Varina, NC 27526-2233; www.weeksdyeworks.com.

Framing

Dot's Frame Shop, 4223A Fleur Dr., Des Moines, IA 50321; 515/285-1994.